698/
859

Skating
elegance on ice

Howard Bass

CHARTWELL BOOKS INC. · Marshall Cavendish London & Sydney

(Previous page) Robin Cousins,
Britain's top free skater.
(Following page) Linda Fratianne,
the petite American lightweight.

Editors
Dorothea Hall
Mary Lambert
Art Editor
Anita Ruddell
Picture Research
Moira McIlroy

Published and distributed by:

Marshall Cavendish Books Limited
58 Old Compton Street
London W1V 5PA
England

IN THE UK, COMMONWEALTH AND
REST OF THE WORLD, EXCEPT
THE UNITED STATES OF AMERICA

ISBN 0 85685 858 7

Chartwell Books, Inc.
A division of Book Sales, Inc.
110 Enterprise Avenue
Secaucus, New Jersey 07094
USA

IN THE UNITED STATES OF AMERICA

ISBN 0−89009−341−5

Introduction

The standard of figure skating is so high today that it is often impossible to predict who will win a particular championship. In previous decades, however, it was easy to forecast the title winners at most international events because there was usually an outstanding performer who would retain a title until he or she either retired from the sport or turned professional. In those days the defeat of a defending champion was a rare occurrence, and a comeback, as in boxing, most unlikely.

Now it is very different. Titles are lost or regained with hardly the raising of an eyebrow, and judges are less inclined to mark champions by reputation. At the 1979 World Championships in Vienna, any of four men and three girls were in sight of singles crowns right up to the last gasp. More men than usual fell in the 'short free' because of the tension of a close conflict. A refreshing wind of change has made wide-open competitions the order of the day, with nerves a key factor. This element of suspense has helped to bring figure skating to the front of television's display case.

Who could imagine, even five years ago, that viewers switching on for a main news bulletin would be kept waiting, for fear of mass protests if a preceding live skating transmission ended before the result was known? This happened on the occasion of the Vienna men's final in 1979, and emphasizes how figure skating has risen in importance on the home screen, affording rich pleasure to many.

As in other sports, it is international competition which grips onlooker and participant alike. So, the genuine enthusiast is justly aggrieved by any form of political interference. I have always believed that unfettered and intelligently organized competitions can promote international goodwill and understanding. To be convinced of this, one has only to observe skaters and other sports competitors happily intermingling behind the scenes of world and Olympic contests. They share obvious common interests and are their countries' finest ambassadors.

This book was visualized largely as a celebration of the beauty of ice skating. Written from an international viewpoint and pitched towards the general reader, the idea has been to explain terminology and be technically descriptive, providing an informative account of the sport's growth and its most prominent performers. With coverage concentrated on amateur competitive figure skating, embracing the four events for men, women, pairs and ice dancing, and also the spectacular by-product, professional theatrical skating, the idea is to promote a fuller understanding and to provide enjoyment for skating's armchair televiewer or rinkside spectator.

The foregoing paragraph summarizes my publisher's 'terms of reference', with encouragement to spice the main ingredients with a sprinkling of personal anecdotes. It is earnestly hoped that all has been suitably fulfilled and that readers thus may derive more pleasure than before when watching surely the most elegant of all sports. If serious participants also become engrossed that indeed will be a welcome bonus.

Howard Bass

Contents

Yesteryears - 6

Evolution and milestones, apparel, equipment and rinks

New Ice Age - 17

The modern skating scene, its expanding appeal and potential

Figuring - 27

The art of tracing figure eights, the basis of technique

Technical Merit - 34

Jumps, spins and other requirements of free skating

Artistic Presentation - 42

Preparing a programme and setting it to music

Pair Skating - 50

Compatibility of partners, pair specialities; judging and scoring

Ice Dancing - 57

International dances on skates; comparison with pair skating

Olympics - 64

The growth of Olympic skating from 1908 onwards

Theatre On Ice - 74

Professional shows on rink, stage, screen and television

Medallists - 82

Comprehensive list of all world and Olympic medal winners

Index - 95

Yesteryears

To feel yourself carried along with the speed of an arrow and the graceful undulations of a bird in the air, on a smooth, shining, resonant and treacherous surface: by a simple balancing of the body and by using only your will as a rudder, to give yourself all the curves and changes of direction of a ship at sea or of an eagle soaring in the blue sky; for me this was such an intoxication of the senses and such a voluptuous dizziness of thought that I cannot recall it without emotion. Even horses, that I have loved so much, do not give to the rider the delirium that the ice gives to the skater.

Alphonse De Lamartine
circa 1830

Somewhere in the Arctic region of northern Europe, one of our ancestors proved a little brighter than his contemporaries. Seeking new territories or a higher standard of living in exchange for the skins from animals he had trapped, he peered across the frozen fjord and pondered on the quickest way to cross it. Spurred, perhaps, by the knowledge that his girlfriend was on the other side, he had a sudden brainwave. Plucking two fairly straight shank bones from a handy reindeer or elk carcase, he ground them laboriously with a piece of flint until each had sharp edges. Binding them to the soles of his feet, he became — no doubt after hurtful trial and error — the world's first skater.

This, or something similar, must have happened at least two thousand years ago, because that is the approximate age of the earliest bone skates in today's museums. One pair, hewn from a horse's cannon-bone, was found bound to the skeleton of a Stone Age man discovered in Friesland, Holland. And another set, made from walrus teeth, was unearthed in Sweden.

The skate, like the ski, was clearly born as a primitive form of transport. The similarity of basic action on either caused early Norwegians to use the same word, *ondur*, for both skate and ski. This resulted in some confusion when translating the earliest writing about either mode of travel, but Scandinavia is believed to be the area of skating's origin. In ancient Icelandic literature, the god Uller is described as remarkable for 'his beauty, arrows and skates', and an old Icelandic poem contains the line: 'Uller, god of winter, runs on bones of animals over the ice.'

The early German word *schake*, meaning a shank or leg bone, *scatch* in old English and *schaat* in Flemish seem together to have produced the modern derivative, skate. As a recreation, skating began to progress on the frozen Dutch canals and, to a lesser extent in England, as early as the eleventh century. A translation from the Latin of William Fitz-Stephen's *Description of London*, published in 1180, contains the following passage:

> When the great fenne or moore (which watereth the walls of the citie
> on the North side) is frozen, many young men play upon the yce . . .
> some tye bones to their feet and under their heeles . . . some stryding
> as wide as they may and shoving themselves by a little picked staffe,
> doe slide as swiftlie as a bird flyeth in the aire, or an arrow out of a
> cross-bow.

The first known illustration of the sport, and early evidence of female participation, is a Dutch wood engraving printed in Brugman's *Vita Lydwina* in 1498. It depicts a skating accident of 1396, when a sixteen-year-old girl called Lydwina from Schiedam in the Netherlands, fell and broke a rib. She entered a convent, where she died in 1433, and, following sanctification in 1890, became known as St Lydwina of Schiedam, the patron saint of skaters.

The wooden skate, with an iron facing, began to make its appearance in the fourteenth century. Archbishop Olaus Magnus wrote in 1555 of this transition when referring to a skater who

> . . . races swiftlie only upon the slippery ice, having a plain [flat surface] of polished iron or plain deer or sheep bones, mainly the shank

Skating on the frozen lakes and canals of Holland (left), has been depicted by many artists since the sixteenth century. This early Dutch winter scene is typical of many and emphasizes how skating became second nature to inhabitants of the Netherlands. It also suggests that European winters used to be harder than they are today.

bones that are naturally slippery by reason of thèir inbred fatness, and are a foot in length, fastened to the bottom of their feet.

The Dutch found their frozen canals the speediest means of travel and it is hardly surprising that artists of the sixteenth and seventeenth centuries made the pastime a subject for their canvases, among them Anthonie Beerstraaten, Isack van Ostade, Cornelius Dusart, Pieter Brueghel and Hendrich Avercamp. Rembrandt, who married in Friesland, sketched a snow and ice scene showing a skater strapping on his skates, and in 1634, he etched a skater with a pole hanging from his shoulder.

Some of the Stuarts who had fled to Holland at the time of the Cromwell uprising returned later to Britain full of praise for the new sport. Indeed, it gained much attention in London during one severe winter, prompting Samuel Pepys to describe in his diary on 1 December 1662, a sight which he beheld that day on the canal in St James's Park: 'Where first in my life, it being a great Frost, did see people sliding with their skeetes, which is a very pretty art.'

On the same day the noted historian, John Evelyn, entered in his diary:

Having seen the strange and marvellous dexterity of the sliders on the new canal in St. James's Parke performing before their maties [majesties] by divers gentlemen and others with scheets [skates] after the manner of the Hollanders; with what swiftness they pass and suddenly they stop in full carrier upon the ice.

Twenty-one years later came London's Great Frost of 1683, which froze the Thames for two months and Pepys danced on the ice with Nell Gwynne. One day that same winter, King Charles II and Queen Catherine arrived on a sled pulled by a skater, to attend an ice gala featuring Dutch sailors.

When the Princess of Orange was escorted on the ice at The Hague by the Duke of Monmouth in 1685, the French Ambassador in Holland wrote in a despatch to King Louis XIV:

'Twas a very extraordinary thing to see the Princess of Orange clad in petticoats shorter than are generally worn by ladies so strictly decorous. These tucked up halfway to her waist, and with iron pattens on her feet learning to slide, sometime poised on one leg, sometime on another.

Pattens was a Flemish word, meaning a pair of skates, and this term was used commonly when skating flourished on the frozen English fens. It bears a similarity to the French *patineur*. The Dutch by this time had become keen on ice racing but the British began to develop a more artistic and recreational element. The world's first skating club was formed in Edinburgh in 1742 and the earliest instructional book, A *Treatise on Skating*, with a text of ten thousand words, was written by an Englishman, Captain Robert Jones of the Royal Artillery, and published in London in 1772. Recounting how the sport was appealing to ladies of high society, Jones observed:

No motion can be more happily imagined for setting off an elegant figure to advantage, nor does the minuet itself afford half the opportunity of displaying a pretty foot . . . A lady may indulge herself here in a *tête-à-tête* with an acquaintance, without provoking the jealousy of her husband; and should she unfortunately make a slip, it would at least not be attended with any prejudice to her reputation.

Grooves or flutes started to appear in the skate at about this time, and people were beginning to talk knowledgeably about the edges of their

blades, which were often flamboyantly curved up and over the toes. Skating had gained favour in the French Court by 1776, when Marie Antoinette became a prominent performer. In 1791, Napoleon, who was then a student at the École Militaire, narrowly escaped drowning when skating on thawing ice over the moat of a French fort at Auxerre.

The German writer, Johann Wolfgang von Goethe, became a keen enthusiast and was perhaps the first to describe skating as poetry of motion. He also observed it as 'an exercise which brings us into contact with the freshest childhood, summoning the youth to the full enjoyment of his suppleness, and is fitting to keep off a stagnant old age, it has no age barriers.' The first book in Germany about skating, *Uber das Schritthuhfahren* by G.V.A. Vieth, was published in 1790. The first French work was *Le Vrai Patineur* by Jean Garçin, published in 1813.

In 1830, The Skating Club — that was its imposing title — came into being in London, its members using the Serpentine lake in Hyde Park when weather allowed. It was somewhat exclusive, with Prince Albert, husband of Queen Victoria, an active patron. One February day in 1841, when the lake at Buckingham Palace froze, his skating zeal nearly cost him his life. The ice cracked and he was shoulder-deep in water when the Queen, then twenty-one, came to his rescue.

Henry Boswell of Oxford, England, in 1837 designed an improved skate for figures, with the blade shortened at the front and lengthened at the back. By this time, British servicemen had done much to popularize skating in the

The Serpentine lake in London's Hyde Park was the scene of numerous skating parties during severe winters of the nineteenth century, when high society enthusiasts of 'The Skating Club' were prominent participants. These included members of the British royal family and members of parliament.

Outdoor skating in the early English style in 1892, when the men wore toppers and tailcoats and the women sported elaborately smart hats and ankle-length skirts. Foursomes and hand-in-hand skating were popular vogues at this time, when club members were often studiously painstaking about technique.

United States and Canada. The first club in the United States was formed in Philadelphia in 1849 and, a year later, a Philadelphia man, E.W. Bushnell, invented the first all-metal skate, both blade and connecting plate being made of iron. It still had to be strapped to the boot, and clamps were devised soon after, which greatly aided precision of movement. The first Philadelphia club skaters regarded elegance of attire with importance and it became the done thing to wear top hats, white ties, swallow-tailed coats and pantaloons.

The first covered rink in North America was erected in Quebec City, Canada, in 1858, followed the next year by the Victoria Skating Rink in

Montreal. These early covered rinks, still with natural ice, made evening sessions and ice galas more practicable and congenial, with modified forms of heating provided for spectators. The New York Skating Club, the second in the United States, was formed in 1860 and from it emerged an American who was to do much to revolutionize the art. Jackson Haines, recognized as the pioneer of the present-day international style of skating, was a professional dancer who sought ways to wed his ballet knowledge to the ice.

Haines travelled in 1864 to Europe, where his exhibitions were warmly welcomed, his new theatrical method being appreciated particularly in Vienna. The originator of the sit spin and the first skater of note to wear a skate which screwed securely to the sole of the boot, his waltzing on ice to Johann Strauss melodies completely won over the Viennese, broadened skating's horizons, and undoubtedly inspired the formation of the Vienna Ice Skating Club in 1867. Symbolic of his popularity was a drawing of Haines which illustrated the score of the waltz in Giacomo Meyerbeer's famous ballet, *Les Patineurs*. 'The American Skating King' were the words inscribed on Haines's tomb at Gamla-Karleby, Finland, where he died in 1875 at the age of thirty-nine.

In the 1870s the female skating attire was still cumbersome, to put it mildly. My contemporary American confrère, Arthur Goodfellow, wrote of: ladies moving over the ice with the stately grace of a schooner under full sail, bundled up like Christmas presents with multi-petticoats, voluminous layers of material, heavy coats, long gloves and high hats. The magazine, *Skating*, founded by the United States Figure Skating Association in 1923, and probably the sport's most respected medium, confirms that the ice fashions of that decade were certainly designed more for warmth than for appearance:

> Women usually wore close-fitting jackets that went to the hips and buttoned down the front—often with a scooped neckline allowing for a scarf or 'Peter Pan' collar and necktie. The skirt was quite full and always worn to the ankle. Underneath was an entire series of petticoats for added warmth. A hat and muff were essential to complete the outfit and give added protection from the chill wind.

The French artist, Henri de Toulouse-Lautrec, in 1880 produced a colourful painting of a 'bundled-up' Parisian female skater, in contrast to to his more familiar scenes inside the theatre.

Serious skating thrived in Scandinavia from the late 1870s, where early great performers were the Norwegian, Axel Paulsen, and the Swede, Ulrich Salchow. Their names still describe the sport's two most celebrated jumps, which they originated. And in England the first artificially frozen rink, the Glaciarium near King's Road, London, was built by John Gamgee in 1876, Its ice surface measured forty by twenty-four feet, and its roof was forty-five feet high in the centre. There were galleries for spectators and the walls were decorated with Swiss alpine and forest scenery painted by Durand of Paris. A larger rink opened in Manchester the following year and others soon began to sprout on either side of the Atlantic.

In Switzerland, the Davos rink opened in 1877, largely through the efforts of British guests at the Hotel Belvedere, and Davos subsequently became the location of skating's international headquarters. Germany's first club was formed at Frankfurt in 1881. But the world's first national organizing body for the sport was the National Skating Association of Great Britain, inaugurated on 1 February, 1879, at the Guildhall, Cambridge. The Association's figure skating committee was formed a year later under the chairmanship of Henry E. Vandervell, who invented the bracket, counter

The skater epitomizes the season in this impression of winter etched in 1885 by E. Gascoigne. The lady appears very sensibly dressed in regard to protection from the cold, though how she could maintain balance without freer use of her arms, is less apparent.

and rocker figures, and was the administrative pioneer of figure skating. His original conception of a graduated system of proficiency tests was later improved and universally adopted through the International Skating Union (ISU).

The United States Amateur Skating Association was formed in 1886 and that of the Canadians in 1887. These organizations were superseded by the United States Figure Skating Association and the Canadian Figure Skating Association, dating from 1921 and 1934 respectively. The ISU was instituted in 1892 at a meeting at Scheveningen, in Holland, attended by six founder members − Austria, Germany, Great Britain, Hungary, the Netherlands and Sweden. Membership has since embraced more than thirty countries.

The Skaters Text Book, published in the US in 1883, daringly recommended the following skating costume:

> Heavy flannels should be worn next to the skin [to absorb the perspiration]. Men and boys should leave off their overcoats and women's and girls' dresses should reach the ankle only. The limbs should be unencumbered for free use and corsets are very injurious during the hours of exercise.

By 1896, London was able to boast three electrically refrigerated rinks. The first was the Niagara Hall, a circular stadium in York Street, near St James's Park; another was the élite Prince's Skating Club in Knightsbridge, and the third was in Argyll Street, near Oxford Circus. The latter was built by Frederick Hengler to house his circus, before being converted to the National Skating Palace, on the site where the celebrated London Palladium Theatre now stands. The development prompted a Canadian, George A. Meagher, to write in his book, *Figure and Fancy Skating*:

> Nature never intended that France and England should be skating countries. That ever-busy and intellectual being, Man, has cheated Nature by the invention of artificial ice, and has lengthened their skating seasons from a period of a few weeks to seven months or more.

The first officially recognized world figure skating championship was held, for soloists only, in Leningrad (then St Petersburg) in 1896. There was then no separate women's event and an early blow for Women's Lib was struck when Madge Syers of Great Britain applied to enter in 1902. There was no rule to say a woman could not compete and, when the organizing committee partly recovered composure, her application was accepted. Indeed, Madge not only entered, but came second to the great Ulrich Salchow, who was so impressed that he gave her his gold medal. However, the ISU congress in 1903 decided that women could not compete again with men. One of the reasons, which would now be described as male chauvinist, was 'that the dress prevents the judges from seeing the feet.'

The National Skating Association of Great Britain responded, somewhat boldly for the time. 'To this we answer that it is impossible to skate the figures properly in a long dress. The dress *must* be short.' This embarrassing situation was resolved by introducing a separate women's championship in 1906, and Madge Syers was a comfortable first victor. The world championship for pairs was added in 1908.

A noteworthy accolade was bestowed on figure skating when events for men, women and pairs gained Olympic status at the Summer Games held in London in 1908. The convenience of the indoor rink of the Prince's Skating Club in the heart of the capital must have been a prime factor. Thus were these the first events of all the snow and ice sports to gain Olympic inclusion,

This outdoor scene (right), depicts an obviously accomplished skating couple, illustrated by Rene Vincent in 1935.

sixteen years before the first separate Olympic Winter Games took place in 1924 at Chamonix, in France.

The early years of this century saw skating spread to distant parts of the globe. Australia's first ice rink, the Melbourne Glaciarium, opened in 1904, and South Africa's in Johannesburg in 1909. In countries less dependent on manufactured ice, the sport at this time reached its outdoor popularity peak. The men wore practical-looking sweaters and jackets with matching caps, while the women's dresses continued to be rather bulky, with feathers and fur in their bonnets becoming increasingly popular.

That competitive figure skating was one of the earliest sports to become properly organized on an international scale may not be entirely unconnected with royal influence. Skating through the years has been a popular recreation of royalty. Czar Alexander II of Russia became a close friend of Jackson Haines and took lessons from him in St. Petersburg. Scandinavian and Dutch monarchs have been noted for skating in public crowds. British royal participants are said to date even from King Harold in the eleventh century. The Duke of Windsor recalled in his memoirs how, when the life of his father, King George V, was slowly ebbing away, Princess Mary was summoned to his bedside. A sharp frost during the night had frozen the pond outside and, as he roused himself, the King asked his daughter whether she had been skating. The Duke wrote: 'My father's mind must have been travelling far back into the past and the wonderful skating parties that he and the rest of us had had there when we were young. Then he dozed off again.' Queen Elizabeth II skated as a child, and both the Prince of Wales and Princess Anne have taken lessons on the Thames-side rink at Richmond.

On indoor rinks, there was evidence of impending fashion changes. The growth of artificial rinks meant that, as chronicler Captain T.D. Richardson observed in his book, *Ice Skating*:

It was possible for the ladies to dress extremely smartly. They wore beautifully-cut black cloth skirts reaching to the top of shining black boots. Now and again there was a glimpse of coloured linings or

A public session during 1910 at the Prince's Skating Club in Knightsbridge, London. The private enterprise of the Duchess of Bedford, this rink was the venue of the first Olympic figure skating competitions, in 1908. It was in a long, narrow hall, with the ice surface measuring 200 feet long by only 50 feet wide. It opened in November 1896 and remained in used until 1917.

petticoats or — very daring — sleek black silk stockings. Transparent chiffon blouses were quite in order — dashing toques with osprey plumes or jewelled brooches made a gay and glittering picture.

But the first sign of the shape of things to come was the occasion upon which one delightful daughter of the aristocracy appeared to give a show one Sunday afternoon — a regular tea-time event, with half the smart world of Edwardian society present — clad in a black silk *maillot* [a turn-of-the-century léotard] atop a daringly short skirt, and quite obviously *no corsets*. This caused the most tremendous sensation and considerable adverse criticism — but she looked so delightful, so graceful and so lissom that gradually a movement for freer clothing for skating began to take shape; but World War I intervened and it was not until peace came again that freedom of costume and movement was finally adopted.

Although the 1920s opened with ankle-length dresses, shorter lengths began to appear until, by 1928, the hemline reached just below the knee. The flowing skirts and petticoats had gone forever.

The 1920s and 1930s were dominated by Sonja Henie, who won three Olympic gold medals and ten world titles before successfully turning professional. I remember, when as a schoolboy, being taken to watch her first feature film. Aptly titled *One in a Million*, it had a very great impact on cinema audiences in 1936. John Logie Baird was yet to give his first public demonstration of television, which I was also fortunate to see at a London theatre, so the very sight of Sonja's fascinating skating was an eye-opener to the millions of movie-goers who had never been inside an ice rink. It is surely no exaggeration to suggest that this film was more beneficial to the worldwide promotion of skating than anything before, and comparable to the present-day effect of televised championships.

According to Sonja the worst *faux pas* of her career was when, at the age of fourteen, she was presented to Queen Mary. She responded to that gracious but formidable lady's disarming expression of interest in the sport with a suggestion that Her Majesty might take up roller skating because it would be less hazardous. The ageing Queen broke the pause which followed, to say: 'I will think about what you have said.'

This remarkable Norwegian gave a tremendous fillip to the fast-growing ice-show profession, which began to blossom brightly and lucratively in the 1930s. Then Hitler rudely interrupted, but skating thrived as never before after World War II. Much shorter skirts and white boots were the order of the day, and it was a time when skating matured and expanded rapidly. Properly organized ice dancing started to flourish and became a fourth event in the World Figure Skating Championships from 1952.

On the morning of 15 February, 1961, when seventy-three people lost their lives as a great Boeing 707 crashed in flames over Belgium, the world of ice skating suffered its most tragic loss, including the whole American team on its way to the World Championships in Prague. That day, one great skating family — a mother and two daughters — was wiped out. Maribel Vinson Owen, who was nine times Figure Skating Champion of the United States and member of three Olympic teams, had been widowed in 1952 and subsequently devoted her major energies to ensure comparable success for her daughters. Notwithstanding the tragedy, it is perhaps slightly consoling to know that she achieved her ambition to see both daughters become national champions, too. Laurence, at the age of sixteen won the United States singles title, and Maribel junior, at twenty-one, won the pairs. This was less than three weeks before they all died. I was privileged to be Maribel's rinkside companion during the Olympic Winter Games at

A poster advertising the Glaciarium, which opened in 1842 in Portman Square, London. Sometimes called the first artificial ice rink, (but somewhat erroneously because its surface, invented by Henry Kirk, was a mixture of alum, grease and ammonia), it was a failure from the skaters' point of view. It was another 34 years before the world's first indoor rink with a satisfactory ice surface opened a few miles away in Chelsea.

15

Sonja Henie, whose example probably influenced the progress of figure and show skating more than that of any other individual. Ten times world champion and Olympic gold medallist at three consecutive Winter Games, the glamorous Norwegian turned professional in 1936, toured extensively with her own ice revue and starred in a dozen full-length skating feature films.

Squaw Valley, California, in 1960, and again during the World Championships which followed that year in Vancouver. I then quickly learned why she was such an exceptionally popular and very colourful character in her sport. That deep-throated voice ardently urging her pupils to extra effort will not be forgotten.

Forgive me for singling out the one I knew best from among thirty-four skaters, trainers, officials and their relatives, whose names throughout that day were telephoned to me by a London newspaper for identification. The shock of the team's loss stunned and saddened the world and the ISU immediately cancelled that year's World Championships.

Indoor rinks did not become obligatory for such championships until after 1967. Aside from the inconvenience and the accidents which occured, this was a sensible decision, for snow could obliterate a figure tracing before judges had time to examine it, and indeed, there was no reason to prolong the lottery of some competitors getting better weather conditions than others. But the most important thing which happened to skating after 1967 was the advent of television coverage, networked in colour to millions of armchair viewers on every continent. Favourable audience research statistics constantly prove how popular it is, whether as a rivetting competitive sport or a glamorous theatrical spectacular.

New Ice Age

(Previous page) A typical present-day scene of an outdoor, public skating session at Mount Royal, Montreal, Canada.

(Below) The world's first successful mechanically frozen ice rink, the Glaciarium in south London, with Alpine scenery decorating the walls. Opened in 1876 by John Gamgee, it was located behind the old Clock House in King's Road, Chelsea. With a skating surface measuring 40 by 24 feet, the ice was produced by a mixture of glycerine and water circulating through copper pipes refrigerated by ether.

Unlike our ancestors, most of us today think of skating, not as a vital means of getting from A to B, but as an intriguing form of movement. As the French say on another subject, *vive la différence*, because it is that aspect which appeals so much. It causes skating, to a greater degree than most other sports, to be a form of escapism. When you go into an ice rink, it is like entering another world, so refreshing is the contrast with everyday life.

The effect it has on confirmed adherents inspires a transformation of a kind which, in my experience, occurs only in one other form of recreation, skiing, and for basically similar reasons. If you travel the last lap of a cog-railway journey with a party of winter sports enthusiasts, winding their way to a mountain resort, as more and more snow becomes visible you will observe their whole attitude changing; a tingling, pent-up excitement welling up to the surface. It is the same when skaters pass through the doors of an ice rink. They become temporarily different, satisfied people in a kind of magical Shangri-La.

Perhaps in tomorrow's more affluent countries, every sizeable urban centre will have at least one rink. But that situation does not yet exist, and present geographical circumstances make the prospect of an early introduction to the sport something of a lottery. The chance which enabled Britain's Robin Cousins to become a famous ice star is a typical example, for when he was young there were no skating facilities near where he lived in Bristol. But at the age of nine, when on holiday with his parents at a summer resort, the family went to a rink, mainly to seek refuge from the heat! This was how Robin became hooked on skating. If it hadn't been for a timely whim, the world may well have been denied such an outstanding performer.

With few exceptions, today's championship-class skaters have never performed in competition on natural ice at any time of their careers.

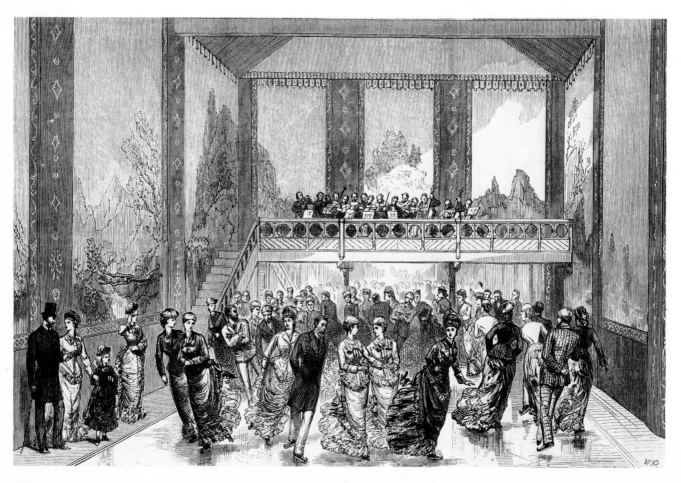

Mechanically frozen rinks have revolutionized the sport beyond the general belief of two or three decades ago. In the early 1950s, you could not find a Swiss ready to predict that an artificial rink would be built at an Alpine resort, a place where natural ice was reliable for skaters during most of the winter. However, the seemingly impossible happened and, as soon as one was installed, a chain reaction set in as winter sports centres clamoured to keep in fashion (rather as English seaside towns had built piers nearly a century earlier). Thirty years ago, the thought of erecting an artificial rink at Arosa , Davos, Grindelwald or Villars was likened to taking refrigerators to Eskimos or sand to the Sahara. But it has happened at all these centres, and many more.

It was not until 1967 that the International Skating Union decreed the World and European Figure Skating Championships must be staged indoors. The decision was not altogether a surprising one, for there were many disastrous outdoor competitions. In 1963, for example, at a men's outdoor event ending after midnight at Cortina d'Ampezzo, high in the Italian Dolomites, every single one of the entrants fell during the free skating because of the hazardous ice conditions. In 1967, in Vienna, the talented Russian pair, Oleg Protopopov and Ludmila Belousova, had to defend their title in decidedly inclement weather. When they and their rivals went on for the preliminary warm-up during torrential rain, Oleg hoisted an enormous umbrella, not only to protect Ludmila and himself, but to underline the foolishness of holding such an important event outdoors when so many covered rinks existed. At the time, the famous French skater Pierre Brunet commented that competitors were not so soft in his day. 'At Chamonix in 1924, when Andrée (Joly) and I won the Olympic bronze medal, there was a blinding snowstorm and it was freezing cold. But we were hardier in those days.'

Spartan they certainly had to be because indoor arenas then were less common, but, if possible, a championship should be not so much a test of hardiness as of technical skill in circumstances as equal and as practicable for all. Inevitably, the element of luck must often have influenced the outcome of events in days when snow could obliterate the tracings of one competitor's figure before the judges could mark it, while a rival's figure could be traced during a clear spell with nothing to disturb concentration. Today, thank goodness, nobody gains or suffers from such widely varying and unpredictable conditions.

The growth of the sport at all levels has been marked since the turn of the century, when the number of permanent rinks in the world could be counted on the fingers of one hand. There are now several thousand in North America alone, and even in South Africa a dozen have been built. In France, there are more than a hundred, some fifteen of them in and around Paris. Most western European nations have expanded in similar vein except Britain, which, although the first to have an indoor rink, has marked time notably in recent years, largely owing to a lack of support or understanding from civic authorities. Greater London, which had three rinks in 1908, astonishingly has never since had more than six in operation at the same time, and has lately fallen below even that sadly inadequate figure for so highly populated an area. The scheduled opening by 1983 of a twin-rink, national skating centre in Manchester is sorely needed in Britain, which has fewer than forty rinks, and several of them are smaller than the ideal size of two hundred feet long by eighty-five feet wide.

The most rapid national expansion in skating has been in Canada, where more than a thousand clubs cater for nearly two hundred thousand active members of the Canadian Figure Skating Association, and these figures represent only a fraction of the people who skate in that country.

There are few age or fitness barriers to recreational skating. Lord Dowding, who was Chief of the RAF Fighter Command during the Battle of Britain, said in his seventy-fifth year, 'At my age, skating is the perfect exercise because you can stop when you have had enough.' And I remember skating on the outdoor Suvretta rink at St Moritz, Switzerland, on a windy, bitterly cold day which eventually sent all of us scuttling to the warmth of a dressing-room — all, that is, except one. She came in more than a quarter of an hour later, and then only after a heavy barrier board had been blown the full length of the rink. 'You are the hardiest of us all,' I commented, which brought the swift response, 'That is because I was brought up tough.' The skater in question was Lady Nancy Astor, at the age of eighty, who years previously had been Britain's first woman Member of Parliament.

Lest the reader think the sport is suitable only for those without a physical handicap, it should be stressed that several star performers first took up skating on medical advice, because of a weakness or deformity. Skating is well known for strengthening weak ankles and developing good posture. It has also helped the physical advancement of polio victims and those with rickets.

A French child who was weakened by wartime malnutrition was told that she would never be able to skate. But she defied such discouragement and strengthened her limbs the more she practised on the ice. Jacqueline du

Jacqueline du Bief, French champion of the world in 1952, who afterwards became one of the most innovative show skaters. Her original ideas and musical interpretation were seen at their best when she starred in ice shows at Wembley, London, in roles like Aladdin and Peter Pan — dramatizing the parts far beyond the normal expectancy of a Christmas pantomime. Such achievements were the more remarkable for a girl who, when an infant, was physically weakened by wartime malnutrition and told she would never be able to skate.

Bief went on to become world champion in 1952 and, for a decade after that, was probably the world's best show skater.

The World Junior Championships of 1979, held in Augsburg, West Germany, produced a girl's title winner, Elaine Zayak of the United States, who lost part of her left foot when she was a baby in an accident with a lawn mower. The boys' silver medallist at the same meeting, Bobby Beauchamp, another American and, incidentally, the first black skater to win a medal in an international championship, was born with a club foot. Both had originally taken up skating as a remedial exercise. In this context, one cannot omit mentioning Harry Whitton, a Londoner who skated for many years without feet. Despite below-knee amputations of each leg, he persevered

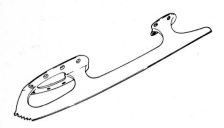

Figure blade

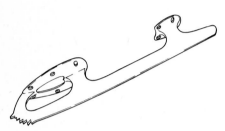

Free skating blade.

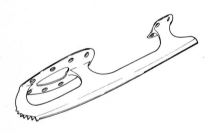

Dance blade

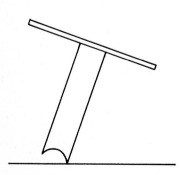

This cross-section of a figure skate shows how the hollow ground blade produces two precise edges.

with artificial limbs until passing proficiency tests both in ice dancing and skiing. Showing me how he fitted skates to the metal legs, Whitton brushed aside my concern about the risk. 'I have an advantage over others,' he smiled. 'I have no ankles to break.'

In Durban, South Africa, group skating tuition for the physically handicapped has been both rewarding and successful. And for blind skaters, too, there has been increased opportunity. Thanks to an admirable Canadian, Margaret Deering, hundreds of unsighted children have learned to skate. The aptly named South-West Vancouver Optimists Club and the Jericho Hill School for the Blind got together to accomplish this remarkable project at the University of British Columbia's Thunderbird Arena. What is more, these very special and courageous pupils improve their posture in the process for a reason Margaret Deering has explained: 'Blind children are frequently round-shouldered because they have no reason to look up, but skating ensures that they keep their backs erect.'

Perhaps the biggest deterrent to making the initial effort to learn to skate is a fear of the unknown. There can be a comparable apprehensive approach to swimming or horse riding, probably for the fundamentally similar reason that each involves a new medium of movement. In all these instances, it takes up to six sessions to adapt to the stage when one no longer feels awkward or not in physical command.

If you had learned to skate, swim or ride at the same time as you learned to walk, you would not have felt any such strangeness. When you learned to walk, although probably you cannot remember, you tumbled about until you found a steady sense of equilibrium. It is just the same with skating. After the first few outings, falls become far less common and one feels more at home and confident. That natural first, self-conscious awkwardness has disappeared, and only countless hours of pleasurable, healthful exercise remain in prospect. It is well worth enduring any early, brief discomfort.

For the average skater, the only equipment required is a pair of boots and skates with protective skate guards. Ordinary, everyday sportswear that is not too loose-fitting is quite suitable for public rink sessions. Only the advanced expert requires more specialized apparel suited to figure or free skating.

Most beginners hire boots with skates attached during their first three or four visits, after which time they usually know whether they are going to like the sport enough to justify buying their own, which, obviously, will be far more comfortable than a rented pair. It is normal to buy a moderately priced pair at the outset and, since the skates are already fitted to the boots, the snug fit of the latter is of major importance. At least half a size smaller than one's street shoes is usually appropriate, because the boot has to fit closely at heel, ankle and instep, though less tightly around the toes.

Only thin socks or stockings should be worn when fitting, because the boot must come to feel part of the foot. In any case, thicker hosiery can hinder circulation and so feel less warm. A new boot fitted over silk or nylon stockings or tights can easily take an ankle sock or woollen stocking later.

All figure skaters, free skaters and, indeed, recreational skaters should wear a figure skate and not a hockey or speed skate. Neither of the latter are welcomed at public sessions by rink managements because they encourage speed and can cause unnecessary danger to others.

The chromium-plated steel figure blade is easily distinguishable from the others by its series of saw-like teeth at the toe end. These teeth are called the toe pick or toe rake and are designed mainly to help spinning and the take-off for some toe-assisted jumps. The underside of the blade is not absolutely straight, but almost imperceptibly curved (a curve usually set on

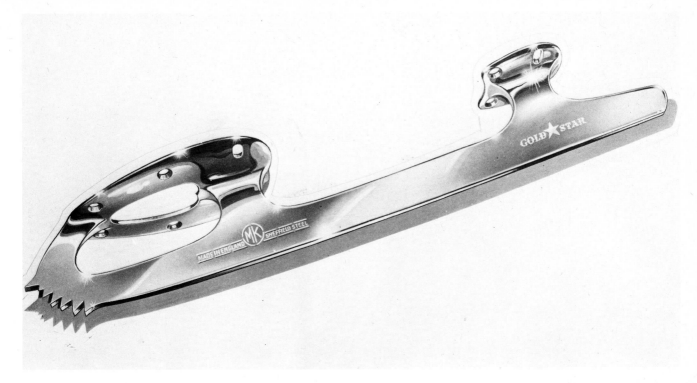

a seven-foot radius).

Fractionally longer than the sole of the boot, the blade is approximately one-eighth of an inch wide. The underside is not flat, but hollow-ground, that is to say fluted along its length to give a hollow, concave ridge. It therefore has two distinct edges, outer and inner, on either of which nearly all skating movements are performed.

Skates have become more specialized for the advanced performer, who may well select a different blade for figures to that used for free skating. There are also blades specifically designed for ice dancing. The figure blade has a shallow, precision hollow grind to minimize double tracking (i.e. skating on both edges together). It has a higher toe pick to avoid catching the ice and marring the tracing. The free-skating blade has a larger toe pick, including a special tooth to afford a good grip in a toe-assisted take-off. The hollow grind is deeper, to minimize slipping, and the blade is side-honed to give even better grip along its edges. All superfluous steel is trimmed off to enhance balance and lightness of weight. The dance blade has a finer edge for intricate high-speed manoeuvrability, and the blade is shortened at the heel to lessen the risk of colliding with the partner's blade during tricky over-lap footwork.

The experienced skater usually prefers to purchase boots and skates separately, because the ideal ready-fixed set to meet a particular preference would be difficult to come by. The blades and boots are afterwards screwed together in a position the skater will have learned suits best. Some prefer the blade to run a little inside the centre of the boot's sole. Many like it to run underneath a point between the big toe and second toe because they believe this position gets the body weight more naturally over the blades.

The blade edges need to be sharpened at periodic intervals, ideally after about thirty hours' use, probably equivalent to a dozen or so full sessions. Skate-grinding is a specialized job, so seasoned skaters learn to make sure their grinder is well recommended by satisfied customers before entrusting their vital equipment to him.

Gloria Nord was once a theatrical roller-skating star who transferred to ice and enjoyed a lengthy reign at the top. After her first ice show had been

A typical example of a modern skating blade in regular use in skating today.

23

Bernard Ford and Diane Towler, four times ice dance champions of the world, always enhanced their appearance by detailed attention to immaculate well-matched costumes. Occasionally ahead of the fashion of their times, they set sartorial trends in the sixties which later became the accepted style.

running a few days, she began to fall in nearly every performance. It was puzzling, until one day I asked if her skates had been sharpened lately. 'Sharpened? You mean they have to be sharpened?' As a former roller skater, she had never been told and certainly learned the hard way, for her blades were truly blunt.

No skater will risk unnecessary damage to the blade edges. That is why all use skate guards, which slip over the blades when off the ice. They are made in such a way as to enable walking on the blades to and from the dressing-room with the guards still on. You will observe that the last thing a skater does before stepping onto the ice is to remove the guards and place them on or beside the barrier or hand them to a friend. The guards will be put on again before or immediately after stepping off the ice.

Just as a musician will care for his instrument, so a skater looks after his boots and skates with painstaking care. The boots, like all forms of footwear, become more comfortable and better moulded to the feet the longer they are worn, so no skater is in a hurry to have to break in a new pair. One also becomes accustomed to the skates and is naturally reluctant to discard an old pair.

Oil smeared on the blades when not in use thus becomes an automatic habit. Boots are cared for by periodic treatment with a non-spirit cleaner that will not damage or dry out the leather. Care is also taken not to leave a pair of skates and boots too near a radiator, because the contrast of temperature could crack the blades or damage the boot leather.

If you see a loose object on the ice, whether it is metal, wood, plastic or paper, any effort made to draw attention to it will be appreciated, be it at a public session or during an ice show or championship, because skaters are very conscious that such objects can cause an unpleasant accident. For this reason, the throwing of floral tributes onto the ice is a deplorable, thoughtless habit not to be encouraged. It holds up proceedings while the ice is scrutinized to make sure that nothing hazardous is left on it to endanger the next performer — to say nothing of obliging the skater concerned to stoop to this indignity while still in a breathless state.

A spill can also be caused through a loose, dangling lace and any skater who has one will appreciate having attention drawn to the fact. Lacing of the boot is a careful ritual for every skater. There are about fourteen pairs of eyelets and hooks on a boot. The skater is concerned to tie the lace loosely at the bottom, to afford ample freedom of movement for the toes. The middle part is laced tightly to give support to the ankle. Above that come approximately six pairs of hooks. The lace is tied tightly around the lowest ones, slightly easier around the next and relatively loosely at the top to allow freer circulation and movement above the ankle. All quite a routine and complicated at first, but simple after a little practice and well worth the trouble. And, there is even an important art concerning the knot. A one-and-a-half bow is found to be neater-looking and more trustworthy than a double bow, and the loose ends are tucked tidily beside the tongue.

Clothing for championship competitors, as much for the recreational skaters, has altered substantially during recent decades, for men as well as for women. It was once quite usual for a male free skater to wear black, until one or two ventured to sport the odd white tuxedo jacket — as eye-opening at first as when Bunny Austin set a precedent by wearing tennis shorts at Wimbledon. Now the close-fitting catsuit is popular. All kinds of colours are acceptable, often with boot covers in shades to match the attire. Sequins or other trimmings are in order, and male pair skaters and ice dancers more often than not wear a colour and style to match that of the partner.

The Royal Albert skate (left), one of two famous presentation pairs made in the nineteenth century for Queen Victoria and Prince Albert by Marsden & Co., each blade being decoratively extended at the toe in the shape of a swan's head. Queen Elizabeth II has since confirmed that there is a photograph in the Royal Family Album of Queen Victoria skating on the same blades.

The modern figure skating boot (right), with skate blade screwed to the sole. Each is sold either separately or comes as a ready-fitted set.

As recently as 1968, the British pair, Bernard Ford and Diane Towler, then World Ice Dance Champions, had expensive, very smart matching costumes in bright orange. They were a sartorial sensation when they appeared in the British Championships that season, their attire meeting with warm approval from an admiring Nottingham crowd. But their national association, not sensing international trends, thought orange too ostentatious and requested them not to wear it for the winter's international events. It was, in my opinion, misguided advice, but the couple reluctantly agreed, only to see rival couples the following year sporting almost identical colours to advantageous effect!

A comparison with tennis is also apt when thinking of the cumbersome long skirts once worn by the women. How on earth could the fair sex cope in tennis with a low backhand drive at full stretch or a sudden rush to the net, and how did a skater manage with a split jump, or spin while grasping one skate above the head? Of course, the degree of athleticism was not so high in those days, and brain probably played a more vital rôle than brawn or flexibility. The modern dress for women free skaters needs to be suited for triple jumps and the positioning of the non-skating leg at any and every angle. Clearly, the skirt has to be cut so that it falls at least several inches above the knee, allowing the fullest possible freedom of movement.

Attractive dresses are an important aspect of presentation at championship level, but the cut and style is more important than the trimmings, now neater and more discreet than during the 1950s, when sequins and rhinestones were predominant. These became less popular when it was realized how disconcerting the dazzle could be on television.

Skaters are expected to be more discreet in their choice of clothing for the compulsory figures. Neat simplicity here is the keynote. A freely fitting tailored dress is very suitable, perhaps with a belt, and long sleeves are favoured if only for warmth, because action is slow. It is prudent to wear a skirt that will not billow out at a time when the judges are watching the tracings and leg movements closely, so the wise wear pleats in the skirt to counter any such tendency.

Skating as a pastime, a sport, an art and a business has spread so widely over the globe, through the development of artificially frozen rinks, that the weather or seasons now negligibly influence its rapidly expanding progress. There is no sign that this popularity may wane and every indication that it will increase. No longer the prerogative of the wealthy and with diminishing difference between the 'peerage and steerage', the trend has transformed traditional ideas of pleasure-going. But what of the future? Will this rate of advancement continue? Is the peak near, or is a decline imminent? My firm contention is that the gathering snowball has hardly begun to roll, that skating is still in its infancy and there is enormous scope for expansion.

However, skating has yet to be recognized in the school sports curriculum on a par with swimming, riding or tennis, although education committees are showing increased interest, with full co-operation in many cases curbed only by a shortage of ice rinks to satisfy potential demand. In the main, civic authorities have been slow to install rinks in fair proportion to swimming pools, but there are signs of a growing general will to correct this imbalance, and the more enterprising have cottoned on to the economic fact that complementary power plants can heat and freeze water in adjacent pools and rinks. Unfortunately, it is of little help to today's would-be young skater to know that his or her ice-starved home town is likely to get a rink in a few years' time. Commuting to the nearest one is not always practical, and so a vast source of potential talent remains untapped.

Figuring

It is ten o'clock on Tuesday morning, the opening day of the World Championships, and the men's compulsory figures have already been in progress for two hours. The spacious, ten thousand-seater ice stadium is almost empty. The smattering of two or three hundred devotees in so large a building does not constitute a crowd.

You enter and, when approaching the rinkside area, you can be forgiven for wondering whether you have come into a cathedral by mistake — inter-denominational, with every creed and colour intermingled as if at a place of common worship. It is the atmosphere, the quietness, the feeling that one should tread gently, if not on tip-toe. If you must converse, it is in a subdued tone or whisper. To cough or sneeze would invite reproving looks, as from a conductor about to raise his baton at a symphony concert. To laugh would seem sacrilegious.

But there is good reason for this, almost reverend behaviour; a shared anxiety, an unwritten rule that one must not divert the attention and break the concentration of the performer, whose every action is being watched intently by nine pairs of discerning eyes — the judges from nine nations — plus numerous other eyes at a greater distance, belonging to knowledgeable coaches, relatives and friends of the contestants, and a handful of the more conscientious representatives of the news media. Apart from official score-keepers, stewards, security staff and, perhaps, a few curious local citizens and the more zealous autograph hunters, that about comprises the attendance — a tiny fraction of the crowds that will throng to the free skating each evening for the rest of the week.

The eyes of every judge watch closely as Sjoukje Dijkstra, of the Netherlands, traces one of the compulsory figures which helped win her third consecutive world title, at Dortmund, West Germany, in 1964. With arms balancing correctly at waist height, she looks over her shoulder to line up the circle while moving in backward direction. For the figures, the judges stand on the ice near each skater, but they sit behind the rink barrier to assess the free skating.

Peggy Fleming, an expert in figures and a proficient all-rounder, gives an exhibition in Boulogne, France. Always calmly composed and delicately graceful, Peggy won the world title three times for the United States, highlighting a memorable amateur career with an Olympic victory in 1968 before starring in a series of widely shown television spectaculars.

In how many sports does such a large proportion of supporters stay away from the first third of a championship? The appeal, however, of the spectacular jumps, fast spins and graceful spirals, coupled with the prospect of a close finish, can fill huge stadiums to capacity and enthral millions of fascinated televiewers. Many past champions have expressed the belief that figures, which must be learned as the solid basic of technique, should comprise no part of a championship at all, and that free skating should be the sole criterion for the judges. Jacqueline du Bief, the French world title holder in 1952, was particularly forthright. She suggested that figures, the way they are emphasized in competition, can actually hurt a skater's free performance and that some of the tedious hours spent in practising figures could be devoted more advantageously to free skating.

The fact remains that figure skating championships are divided into three sections: the compulsory figures, which are worth thirty per cent of the total marks; short free skating, in which each entrant has to perform and link seven specified movements within two minutes, worth a further twenty per cent; and the final free skating, five minutes for each man and four for women, which accounts for the remaining fifty per cent.

Why are figures included? A good question. Tracing figures is the basic means of learning to skate firmly and smoothly, with correct posture and style, on either edge of the skate in forward or reverse direction. Without first learning figures, it is said the quality of free skating would degenerate until future championships were reduced, as one expert put it, 'to a series of clowns cavorting across the ice'.

Even if this were true, is it reason enough to include figures in a championship? A top-class skater is assumed to be proficient in figures anyway. Why test the figures separately in a major contest any more than one would test a tennis player in lobbing or serving, or a golfer in driving or putting? The commonest response is because otherwise the temptation would be too great to neglect figures in training and concentrate almost entirely on free skating — learning to run before you can walk, or, in this case, to jump and spin before you can hold a steady spiral.

In spite of this, are figure eights really on the way out? I pose the question because rumour has it so, and the general concensus of opinion, among the leading ISU officials with whom I have discussed the matter, is that the eventual removal of figures is inevitable. But it is thought by most administrators that a package condition for dropping them from championships must be some new system to ensure that an acceptable standard of ability in figures need still be reached in order to be allowed to compete. That is the crux. Throughout the past thirty years, it has been constantly argued that figures are not what the general public want to see. Dick Button, of the United States and a former world champion, once likened their inclusion to an imaginary golf championship, where part of the competition 'consisted merely of the usage of standard clubs in shots chosen by lot — and done in triple repetition.'

It now seems likely that figures will be outvoted during the early 1980s — but probably only for senior championships. It would be logical to retain them in junior contests. For seniors, their elimination would depend on general agreement concerning a comprehensive plan to safeguard the maintenance of a required ability in figures.

The answer will probably be a special test which all skaters would have to pass before entering a championship. An internationally judged test would be needed, rather than the acceptance of national proficiency certificates, which lack uniformity. Only on such a condition would the abolition of figures from senior championships be acceptable to most member nations of

Lacing the boot is a work of art in itself. It has to be tight in some places and looser in others, to ensure proper control and comfortable circulation. Making sure hers are correctly adjusted is Carol Heiss, whose consistent figures and equally reliable free skating gained five consecutive world titles and an Olympic gold medal for the United States.

the ISU. It should be stressed that it is not the obligation to practise figures which is now in question, but only their continued inclusion in those events most dependent on spectator appeal.

Nearly every movement on skates is made on either of the blade's two edges. Figures teach and test control and style when circling and turning on the inner or outer edge of each blade, in forward or reverse direction. There is an international schedule of forty-one compulsory figures. Twenty-eight may be skated clockwise or anti-clockwise, which makes a total of sixty-nine variations. From all these, three are drawn by lot and skated in a senior championship. They are exercises designed to provide the best technical groundwork for proficient skating. They teach the ability to maintain slow movement and changes of direction on one foot by dint of correct body weight transference and appropriate positioning of the arms and non-skating leg. Hence, they are called either school figures or, because they are obligatory in competitions, compulsory figures.

As already indicated, too much detail would tend to bore all but the connoisseur, so suffice here to select some main differences and terms which

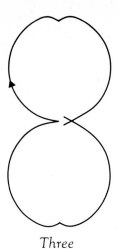

Three

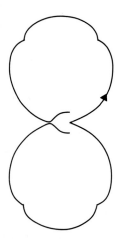

Double Three

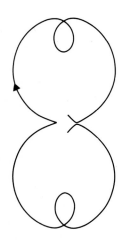

Loop

Cecilia Colledge, one of the best tracers of figures the world has seen, with her Swiss mentor, Jacques Gerschwiler—a combination which led to the world title for Britain in 1937 and a close second place to Sonja Henie in the 1936 Olympics.

should enable the casual onlooker to watch with clearer appreciation of what compulsory figures are really about.

Each figure comprises two or three adjacent lobes, thus looking either like a figure eight (two lobes) or an eight with an extra lobe adjoining. When executing a figure, the performer leaves a tell-tale etching on the ice, called a tracing. Each figure is skated three times without stopping, the second and third tracings being superimposed as closely as possible over the first tracing. The figure is begun from a stationary position, with no possibility to gather initial momentum. Two cardinal sins in this exercise, rare at senior level and appropriately penalized, are skating at any time on the flat of a blade instead of an edge (this would leave a double track mark like tiny railway lines), and touching down, i.e. putting the non-skating foot on the ice.

The skater is judged not only by the accuracy of the visible tracings laid down, but by the style of execution. In a sense, they are integrated, because the correct positioning of hands, head, arms and non-skating foot assist a better tracing anyway. The maintenance of a smooth, steady speed without jerking or rushing, and the precision of turning on one foot or changing from one to the other, as required, are all assessed meticulously.

Posture plays a vital rôle, with head held upright, eyes looking between two and three feet ahead of the skating foot; body erect from the waist up,

yet suitably flexed for rotation. The free leg has to be slightly bent and allowed to swing freely from the hip, with toe pointed in downward and outward direction. The arms should be held outwards at about hip level but below the waist, with the forward palm downwards and the rear palm inclined at an angle, with thumb uppermost. Fingers should be kept straight and closed, without fanning. The diameter of each circle or lobe in the figure ideally should be about three times the skater's height.

The main variations in the type of figure are the three, double three, loop, bracket, rocker and counter. These are summarized here as briefly as possible.

A three is a turn executed on one foot, involving both a change of direction and a change of edge. It is so named because the tracing it leaves simulates an elongated number three.

A double three comprises two such turns placed on the same circle of a figure, each at one-third the distance of the circle.

A loop is a small eliptical loop inscribed within a circle, both loop and circle being skated on one continuous edge of the same foot.

A bracket is a half-turn from one edge to the other of the same blade, performed so that the skater remains within the circle, leaving a tracing with the point of the turn facing outwards from the circle (opposite to the shape made three tracing).

A rocker is a turn involving a change of direction without changing the edge at the point of the turn.

A counter is a half turn, which also enables a change of direction on the same edge of the blade.

More comprehensive figures, preceded by the word 'paragraph', indicate that the full figure eight is performed on the same skate, instead of making a transitional change of feet at the starting point, which is in the centre of the eight.

The observer can quickly appreciate that the slow tempo of compulsory figures and the painstaking method of their execution are particularly suited to a calm temperament. Patience and unflustered concentration are required. Conversely, the daring jumps and spins of the free skating demand an opposite, more fiery and adventurous spirit. That is why the majority of skaters are, by virtue of their nature, notably better at one or the other. One could say that the requirement of differing temperaments is in itself a challenging test of character and adaptability.

In consequence, many outstanding free skaters have to spend the lion's share of their training time concentrating more on figures, to bring these up to their free-skating standard, or vice-versa. The champion needs to be a versatile all-rounder under today's regulations, but in the past the rules tended to favour the better figures exponent, because a greater proportion than now of the total marks could be amassed in that section.

Probably the best performers of figures I have seen are Cecilia Colledge, Jeannette Altwegg, Patricia Dodd, Carol Heiss and Trixi Schuba, all women. It is no coincidence that the first three named are British, because two London-based Swiss coaches, Jacques Gerschwiler and his half-brother, Arnold, have been outstanding tutors in this department. The former, known to all as 'Gersch', made Cecilia, his first pupil and she, in turn, made him, in the sense of world renown. Cecilia, world champion in 1937, then star of ice shows before herself settling to coach in Boston, Massachusetts, for at least twenty-five years, has spent more hours of her life on the ice than anyone else I know.

'Whatever is done should be done beautifully,' Cecilia once said to me, a philosophy echoed later by John Curry. Many other skaters are, like these

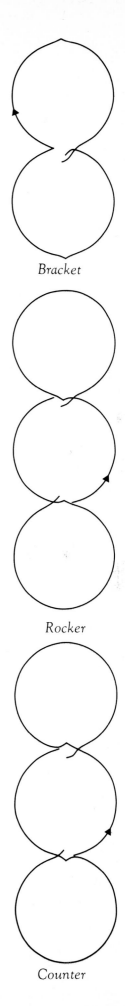

Bracket

Rocker

Counter

Trixi Schuba, of Austria, is generally regarded as the outstanding figure tracer of all time. Her strength in figures was underlined by her relative weakness in free skating, but she amassed a lead formidable enough in the compulsories to be able to stay ahead overall, thus winning two world titles as well as an Olympic crown.

Aja Vrzanova, the first Czechoslovak skater to win the women's world title, in 1949 and 1950, was an unflappable figure tracer who never allowed her concentration to be disturbed. Her long limbs were used to good effect, as in this graceful spiral. In the United States, she shortened her name to Zanova before embarking on a successfull ice show career.

two in particular, perfectionists at heart, and will strive to accomplish what they do as near to textbook technique as they can. To do it beautifully is something more. It means elegance on ice.

Jeannette Altwegg, also coached by Gersch in her final seasons, was so conscientious that anything she put her mind to had to be done well. Had she not concentrated on winning an Olympic gold medal in 1952, she might well have become Wimbledon tennis champion instead. I saw her narrowly lose in the final of a Junior Wimbledon, at which point she had to choose between two sports, because each sport really required her undivided attention. Jeanette was brilliant at figures, ending with sufficient marks in hand to maintain an overall lead after relatively weak free skating.

Patricia Dodd was perhaps the most unflappable. During one championship, while she was tracing figures with customary studious application, a friend remarked: 'If a grenade exploded at the other end of the rink while Pat was in the middle of a figure, she would not even hear it, but complete the tracing — and someone would tell her afterwards what had happened.'

By the time Carol Heiss had won the Olympic gold medal at Squaw Valley, California, in 1960, hers was very much a household name in North America. She went on to win the world title for a fifth time at Vancouver a fortnight later. Whilst standing in the foyer of the Vancouver rink, the Capilano, I was approached by a young reporter from a local newspaper, who asked if I knew Carol because he wanted to arrange an interview. Receiving an affirmative reply, the blissfully innocent reporter exclaimed: 'Oh, good. where is *he*? A *faux pas* like that can stay in one's memory for a lifetime.

Trixi Schuba's figures were so good that her commanding margin at the end of the compulsories enabled her to win two world titles and an Olympic gold medal in spite of embarrassingly sub-standard free skating. It was somewhat of an anti-climax to see this tall Viennese girl free skating with relative mediocrity at the 1972 World Championships in Calgary, Canada. Her performance was adequate for overall victory only because of her tremendous advantage amassed in the figures. Never had a gold medallist relied so heavily on figures and never would it happen again, because of the new rules which became effective the following season, and no doubt spurred by her 'lop-sided' performances, reduced the proportion of marks for figures, and their number from six to three. But Trixi's shortcomings as a free skater must not detract from the accolade due to the most brilliant exponent of figures the world has seen.

In recent years, judging panels have revealed extraordinary discrepancy between their markings of the figures and the free skating. Why the highest mark for figures is usually around four-point-five out of six, when five-point-eight and more is frequently awarded for jumps and spins, has never been satisfactorily explained. This apparently deliberate downgrading of the figures is wholly unjustified.

Weird, unwieldy-looking contraptions seen during practice sessions for figures — but no longer during the warm-up for a championship, when they are barred — are devices like schoolboys' geometric compasses on a giant scale. They are called scribes and are used during figure training to mark out circles of desired radius. Some coaches swear by them, others swear at them. Those in favour aver that they greatly assist the skater in learning the required measurement of the arcs; those against say that they make the pupil too dependent on a scribe, making them feel like a fish out of water when without one in a championship warm-up, and that they mar the skater's ability to calculate the right dimensions without mechanical aid. Whoever is right, there is no doubt that you have to watch where you tread to avoid tripping over these cumbersome gadgets at rinks when figure tracing is in progress.

The relationship between coach and pupil is of crucial importance to a skater's success. A good instructor in any sport must have an adaptable manner and be diplomatic enough to be sharp and stern with those who thrive on such an approach, to coax gently and quietly others who respond better to such treatment, to be witty with those with a ready sense of humour, to avoid showing impatience, and so on. Temperaments must integrate and mutual respect must exist; otherwise, the two should part company before progress is damagingly retarded.

The pupil needs to trust the coach implicitly in order to obey every instruction with confidence. This kind of discipline can be, and often is, undermined — to the pupil's detriment — by thoughtless intervention in the relationship from well-meaning parents. For example, if a tutor says 'be in bed by nine tonight' on the eve of a championship, it should be regarded as tantamount to an order. If a parent knowingly countermands it by saying 'you can watch the TV serial at ten', this can damage the instructor's vital disciplinary control. But if sufficient mutual respect exists, the coach's wish will be the pupil's command.

Harvard-educated Dick Button, with his ready sense of humour, once praised the inspired talent of his Swiss instructor, Gustave Lussi, with this comment: 'Should he have told any of his pupils to jump out of the window, they would have done it. But each would have done it with his toe pointed and his head in the right position to get the maximum clearance.'

Most top instructors enjoy this kind of unquestioning obedience. Carlo Fassi, who, with his wife, Christa, has built an almost unique finishing-school for champions at Denver, Colorado, not only commands unwavering respect from his star pupils, but has the commendable capacity to nurture a genuinely friendly relationship among them, even if they are deadly rivals in competition.

Carlo really does not have the time to deal with performers only halfway up the ladder, and maybe would not be so good at handling them, but his speciality was once aptly described by a fellow professional, Fritz Dietl: 'Other instructors do the car-washing; Carlo does the Simonizing.'

Jeannette Altwegg had an ideally calm temperament to suit the patience required for consistent accuracy in figures. Like so many gifted figures exponents, her free skating was less strong. Despite this, she became Britain's world champion in 1951 and Olympic gold medallist the following year.

33

Technical Merit

Free skating is the visually exciting, more spectacular part of the sport — comprising, in the main, jumps and spins with spirals and linking steps. A free skating performance is one in which these elements are joined together in a technically suitable sequence.

Linking steps is a self-explanatory term. Spirals are long glides, usually on one edge of either blade, in forward or reverse direction, while the body is held in a sustained pose. The clearest definition of a spiral is a moving statue, and it can be readily appreciated how a sustained glide on one edge is born from the technique of tracing figures. There are many kinds of spiral positions, and some new ones, no doubt, remain to be discovered. The commonest is a forward glide on a bent knee, with the non-skating leg extended high behind and the arms stretched out, parallel to the ice. There are numerous variations of this.

The spreadeagle, with heels together and toes pointed in opposite directions, is really a two-footed spiral. A well-held spreadeagle can look very graceful, and is a neat way to describe a full semi-circle at one end of the rink. Each skater develops his or her own best spirals, which will vary among individuals according to physique. Some positions are more suited to long legs, and so on. One skater, according to personal build, may look better than another in a particular pose and so each learns to concentrate on the kind which suits best.

Whereas each compulsory figure is awarded only one set of marks out of six from each judge, two sets of marks, each out of six, are given for free skating — the first for technical merit and the second for artistic presentation. The more difficult the technical contents are in a performance, the more marks a skater will receive, provided of course that they are performed correctly. The second set of marks are more an assessment of the manner of performance, so this chapter explains some of the main technical points to look for and the following chapter deals with their artistic presentation.

Sometimes a skater will be described as spinning well to a centre. This means that the spin is being executed as nearly as possible on one spot, without undue 'travel'. The more the travel, the less correct the spin. An essential of a one-foot upright spin, once the turn is begun, is to keep the skating knee rigid. Since both arms and the free leg are gradually drawn in close to the body, if the spin is a good one, hardly any motion should be discernible during the rotation until the non-skating foot is carefully lowered near the spinning ankle, a process which increases the momentum. To achieve true symmetry, it is necessary to keep the shoulders level while rotating. The head must be held erect, and the skater should look neither down, nor up, but keep a level gaze throughout. When performed correctly, the body will not rock and the skater will not feel dizzy, though a swimmy sensation is temporarily experienced by beginners until they have learned, by correct positioning, how to avoid rocking. As the speed of the spin slackens, the rotation is finally arrested by drawing the free leg away from the skating knee and touching the toe pick of the free foot on the ice, at the same time raising the arms to check the shoulder movement. I often quote Sonja Henie's idea of adding a distinct toss of the head at the end of a spin. This, she said, not only looks effective, but, 'it clears the cobwebs, too'.

A bird's-eye view of Barbara Ann Scott in a lay-back spin, with head well behind her shoulders and arms at full stretch. Barbara Ann was twice world champion and, in 1948, became Canada's first Olympic gold medallist. Later, as a professional, she thrilled London ice show audiences in the title role of 'Rose Marie'.

The three really good spins you are sure to see in any top-grade contest are the camel spin, the sit spin and the cross-foot spin. The camel spin, alternatively called the arabesque spin, resembles in appearance the arabesque in ballet. The distinctive features to recognize are the body and free leg parallel to the ice, with back arched. The arms are held in several different positions to give varying effects.

The sit spin, one of the commonest seen but the most difficult to perform really well, is easy to identify because here the skater adopts a sitting posture. It starts in the upright position, the performer then sinking on to the skating knee, with the non-skating leg extended in front. It is necessary to pull the stomach well in and to bend the body well forward during the lowering process. A pronounced forward lean during the spin is not simple, but this can add much to the effect. Robin Cousins, probably the best-ever exponent of the sit spin, has achieved this lean to admirable advantage, even to the extent of lowering his head quite close to the ice — not nearly so easy an operation as he has made it appear.

The cross-foot spin, the fastest and most impressive, is a two-foot spin well favoured to end a programme. It is a crowd-pleaser and, if well executed, a sudden finish on the spot after such rapid gyrating can bring any solo programme to an appropriate climax. Both knees have to be rigid during this spin. The toes of both feet are close together. A sudden burst of

A perfectly poised lay-back spreadeagle on the outside edge of each blade, performed by the East German, Anett Pötzsch, who became world champion in 1978, fulfilling abnormal promise displayed years earlier. Another of her specialities has been the triple salchow jump, which she first accomplished in international competition when only 13.

speed at the end can be achieved by clasping the hands together, but a really skilful performer can increase the dramatic effect by raising one or both hands above the head during this spectacular movement.

Spinning in recent years has become a relatively neglected art, at least among men, as greater emphasis on higher and more difficult jumps has been introduced. Generally speaking, women have thus become rather more noted for their spinning qualities. A spin can be very elegant and surely nobody has made one look more so than the American skater Peggy Fleming. There was a long lapse in really good male spinning after the great Austrian exponent, Emmerich Danzer, retired from competition in 1968. But, happily, the art is now becoming more fashionable, judges tending to hint by their marks that a performance can be overloaded with jumps, however, difficult they may be. You can have too much of a good thing, and these days there is a demand for a return to greater versatility.

But jumping is, nevertheless, naturally destined to dominate the skating scene because it is so thrilling to watch. Each year, the top performers somehow manage to achieve greater elevation, and the proportionately increased element of risk captures the onlooker's admiration. A good jump depends so much on the art of timing. The spring is made from the skating leg, and the rotation of the body during the jump is effected by pulling the arms inward. To gain maximum possible height, it is necessary to concentrate on forward, upward projection before starting to rotate.

A fundamental jump, often used in conjunction with others, is the three jump. This involves skating forwards on the outside edge of either blade and making a half-turn in the air before landing, in backward direction, on the outside edge of the opposite blade to that used for the take-off. The landing should be effected on the front (toe) part of that edge while travelling backwards. If not, a harsh, give-away scraping sound will be heard.

Most jumpers prefer to rotate in an anti-clockwise direction, taking off from the left foot and landing on the right, but if it does come more naturally to rotate clockwise and take off from the right foot, so be it. The bent skating knee straightens and the spring is made just as the free leg passes the skating foot. The skating knee has to bend when landing, and the landing is made with the free leg extended behind.

All jumps are identified by names and basic differences between each kind of jump are the edges used for take-off and landing. This at first may seem confusing to the non-skating onlooker, but the enthusiastic spectator soon likes to try and differentiate between jumps and the following is intended to help the average spectator to recognize the different jumps.

The split jump is the easiest of all to spot because here the skater adopts a near-horizontal, split-legs posture in the air, with arms stretched out in line with the legs. The skater takes off in backward direction, usually from an inside edge of either blade, with assistance from the toe point of the free blade. A half-turn is executed in the air while in the splits position, before landing in forward direction on the inside edge of the opposite blade to that used in take-off.

Whether incredibly fast detail within jumps can be followed or not, the splits position is clear for anyone to see. Not all the best skaters attempt this one because it is one of those movements which come more easily to some than others, according to their physical build rather than their technical know-how. To those with a suitable build, it is a relatively simple jump, but worth performing because of its showy, pleasing effect.

Four important jumps, each involving a complete mid-air rotation, are the loop, salchow, lutz and walley. Each is approached in backward direction, so it does take a certain amount of experience to distinguish them early

Donald Jackson (left) of Canada, the greatest free skater of his day, is best remembered for an outstanding 1962 world title win in Prague, where he merited a double entry in the Guinness Book of Records — the first to accomplish a triple lutz jump and the skater to receive the highest number of sixes from the judges. Ten years later, he remained in constant demand for exhibitions throughout the world.

Jan Hoffmann, the East German world title winner in 1974, proved a consistent all-rounder by finishing among the top three on six occasions in seven years — the missed year being when a knee injury kept him on the sidelines for a whole season. One of the least vulnerable to competition pressure, Jan has seldom failed to produce his best.

and accurately. The following essential differences may help identification.

The loop jump starts from an outside edge take-off, landing also in backward direction on the same edge of the same blade. This jump may not be particularly high, but covers an appreciable distance.

The salchow jump, created by the Swede, Ulrich Salchow, starts from an inside edge take-off, landing backwards on the outside edge of the opposite blade. A tell-tale sign of a salchow jump on the way is the forward outside three turn used in the approach. The jump is higher than the loop in relation to distance covered.

The lutz and walley jumps are the only ones performed in reverse rotation, i.e. clockwise instead of the normal anti-clockwise. The lutz approach is fast, with skating knee bent extra low. The take-off is from an outside edge, with the free toe used as a lever. The backward landing is made on the outside edge of the opposite blade to that used for the take-off. The over-the-shoulder look immediately before take-off is particularly pronounced and the feet are kept noticeably close during rotation.

Named after its American creator, Nat Walley, the walley jump backward take-off is from an inside edge, with backward landing on the inside edge of the same blade (the same feet, but opposite edges to a loop, and with reverse rotation).

A toe salchow jump, alternatively known as a flip jump, is like a salchow jump, but with take-off toe assistance from the free foot. Likewise, a toe loop jump, also called a cherry flip, or cherry, is a loop jump with take-off toe assistance from the free foot.

Last but not least of the main jumps, and certainly the most famous, is the axel jump, originated by the Norwegian, Axel Paulsen. Usually more recognizable if only because of the prolonged height attained, it involves one-and-a-half mid-air rotations. Really a three jump and loop jump combined, its imminence is easier to predict during a performance because of the forward approach with a well bent knee. The take-off is from an outside edge and the backward landing is made on the outside edge of the opposite blade.

These are single jumps. Double jumps are precisely the same but with an extra mid-air rotation, while triple jumps involve two extra rotations. The double axel therefore includes two-and-a-half turns and the most difficult triple axel, the newest to be accomplished, three-and-a-half turns. A jump does not count as having been performed if the skater fails to land one-footed on a true edge without either falling or touching the ice with a hand.

An idea of the degree of difficulty of each jump can be gained from its ISU factor, a value for judges' reference. By this rating, the higher the factor, the more difficult the jump.

Name of jump	Factor	Name of jump	Factor
loop	2	double loop	5
toe loop	2	double toe salchow	5
salchow	2	double toe walley	5
toe salchow	2	double lutz	6
toe walley	2	double axel	7
axel	3	triple salchow	7
lutz	3	triple loop	8
walley	3	triple toe loop	8
double toe loop	4	triple lutz	8
double salchow	4	triple axel	10

The first triple jump ever to be accomplished in international competition was the triple loop, by the American, Dick Button, who included one in the 1952 Winter Olympics in Oslo. Button has the unique distinction of having held, in 1948, five major titles concurrently. He was World Champion five consecutive times, from 1948 to 1952; Olympic gold medallist twice, in 1948 and 1952; North American Champion three times, in 1947, 1949 and 1951 (open to American and Canadian skaters, but no longer contested); United States Champion seven times, from 1946 to 1952; and European Champion in 1948, the last occasion when the latter was open to Americans.

'The triple loop jump was the most formidable challenge I faced,' Dick wrote afterwards. 'It was a task which was physically painful and mentally frustrating. At times, in desperation, I was almost ready to concede that the jump was beyond my achievement.'

The unusual stress strained the ligaments of his left leg only weeks before the Games, causing curtailment of precious practice time. The jump's eventual accomplishment in Oslo was much heralded by advance publicity. This was intentional, Dick and his trainer, Gus Lussi, having agreed that if the judges were not forewarned as to what to look for, the feat might not be recognized. As Dick later commented: 'We feared they might well have asked themselves whether it was a triple revolution or an optical illusion.'

The first triple lutz did not come until 1962, when the Canadian, Donald Jackson, included one in his world championship victory that year in Prague. Don's Toronto instructor, Sheldon Galbraith, first broached the subject during the preceding summer. After Don had accomplished the jump five times in practice by Christmas, they planned to include it in the Canadian Championships, but he two-footed the landing, which hardly heightened confidence for attempting it in a world meeting.

Harvard-educated Dick Button, seen here in a sit spin, heralded a new era of athleticism in men's free skating during the late forties. The first person to achieve a triple jump – the triple loop in 1952 – he won five world titles, two Olympic gold medals and seven successive United States championships. He has since remained in the public eye as a skating commentator on American television.

Vern Taylor of Canada was never particularly prominent in international contests until, during the 1978 world championships in Ottawa, he became the first skater to achieve a triple axel jump — a mighty leap involving three-and-a-half mid-air rotations. This most difficult triple has prompted belief that landing a quadruple jump in a championship, probably a quadruple salchow, may soon become a reality.

As the time drew near, they began to wonder if its inclusion was really necessary. If he could win without it, why risk possible injury if it was missed in what otherwise might be a flawless programme? When it comes to the crunch, the skater really decides at the last moment about the inclusion of the most difficult and therefore riskiest contents. It must depend, inevitably, on how one feels at the time and how the competition situation pans out. 'If in doubt, leave it out' is a tempting maxim at the eleventh hour, but Don felt on top form and determined to have a go as he laced up his boots. Any final hesitation was resolved by the realization that an exceptional effort was required to overhaul his Czechoslovak rival, Carol Divin.

What happened is now a most glorious part of skating's history. Don not only pulled off the triple lutz, he made it merely the highlight of what many still insist has been the best five minutes of free skating ever performed. Certainly it received the highest number of maximum six marks ever to be awarded to a soloist — no fewer than seven sixes for a display hardly short of perfection.

The first triple axel was achieved by Vern Taylor, another Canadian pupil of Galbraith, at the 1978 World Championships in Ottawa. It was an electrifying moment. Vern had not done well in figures and therefore had nothing to lose by trying a jump which we knew he had accomplished during training.

I watched very carefully. Responsible for annually updating the winter sports sections in the *Guinness Book of Records*, it was necessary to be sure if the three-and-a-half rotations were properly completed and the jump correctly landed. The answer was apparent by the instant reaction of more than a score of the world's greatest technical experts, the top-grade instructors, who, to a man, rose to give a standing ovation.

Had there been any doubt in their minds, these would have been the last to give false credit. My situation was remarkable. Sitting beside me was Don Jackson and a few yards in front of us was Dick Button, acting as television commentator. I quickly asked both in turn if the landing was worthy of being recorded as the first-ever triple axel. Who better qualified to answer? We all agreed that the landing was a little unsteady, but that it was effected correctly on a true back outside edge of the blade, and that three-and-a-half rotations indeed had been made. To add the seal of officialdom, the ISU afterwards showed a film of it and pronounced it to be valid.

The question of physical limits to sporting endeavour was revived with a new slant following the men's event of the 1979 World Championships in Vienna. Many falls from triple jumps fired speculation about the effect of such tremendous leaps on the human body. One veteran coach commented: 'This is too much. They get higher every year. Where will it end? Triples should be banned before the matter gets out of hand and someone gets maimed. An obsession for multiple jumps is taking too much attention from spins and other skating skills.'

To many, curbs on triples would seem as sacrilegious as lowering the wall in show jumping, or narrowing Becher's Brook in the Aintree Grand National. One recalls when, in track athletics, Sidney Wooderson's world mile record stood at four minutes, six-point-four seconds. At the time Harold Abrahams, that great athletics statistician, thought nobody would ever break the four-minute barrier. Soon after, in 1954, Roger Bannister did so, the feat became almost commonplace and two hundred and eighty-five athletes had followed suit by the landmark's twenty-fifth anniversary in 1979.

A parallel is happening in skating. The 1978 accomplishment of the first triple axel had long been thought impossible. Yet Sheldon Galbraith, who taught Vern Taylor how to do it, says skaters will be doing quadruples

within a few years. But at what physical cost? Robin Cousins and Jan Hoff-mann are probably the two most powerful jumpers the sport has known. It is perhaps no coincidence that cartilages have been removed from both the knees of Cousins and from one of Hoffmann's. Each has landed more comfortably and with apparently less risk of further injury since these operations. The jolt to muscles and tissues each time a skater lands from a height on unresilient ice is entirely different from the cushioned surface provided for a high-jumper or pole-vaulter in athletics.

When watching recent world junior championships, with an age limit of sixteen for soloists and quite a lot of triples to be seen even at this level, one could not help wondering, perhaps a little facetiously, how many of these most prominent younger skaters will eventually lose their cartilages. A specialized medical adviser to the ISU says that one can jump high with fewer injury hazards after losing knee cartilages, but that only those who stay physically active in later life may escape subsequent rheumatic or arthritic problems. Could it become one day the done thing to have them out? Surely not, but enquiries have produced a sobering thought.

Britain's Robin Cousins, the world's best-ever free skater, has made triple jumps and fast spins look deceptively easy. More than that, he developed an artistic form of presentation and musical interpretation which helped set exciting new standards for future skaters to follow. Injuries from the continual physical strain of high jumping never diminished his ardour and time and again he showed a really remarkable resilience when rapidly recovering from inopportune mishaps.

41

Artistic Presentation

The engrossing end-product of figure skating is the free-skating performance, a demonstration not merely of technical skills but of artistic creativity. Its preparation is absorbing and the finished article reflects the skater's individual personality.

The skater who can perform a reasonable selection of the technical elements described in the previous chapter faces the exciting challenge of arranging them in the most attractive possible order and linking them suitably together; the whole performance is timed and intelligently interpreted to appropriate music chosen for its mood and rhythm.

Put this way, artistic presentation sounds a pretty tall order, and indeed it is. A labour of love, certainly, but very time consuming. Composing such a programme, which lasts five minutes for men and four for women, takes months of careful planning and painstaking practice. And a skater tunes his performance to concert pitch, pacing training to reach peak form on the big day. If, after such diligent preparation, a fall or other blatant error mars the score, it is hardly surprising when the luckless individual concerned becomes emotionally upset and wants to crawl away into privacy.

That is the harder side, but most competitors believe such risk to be worthwhile, knowing perfectly well that one cannot always win, that experience of defeat can be a valuable teacher, and that everything may come right another day. There are some who think desperately in terms of winning (second place means failure), but the majority derive exhilaration and satisfaction from taking part, irrespective of the outcome.

It is sobering to reflect that all world championship competitors are amateurs. Training at top level will probably cost their parents a small fortune which many can ill afford. A large number of participants come from humble homes, and often a father has undertaken part-time work in addition to his normal job, to keep his son or daughter in training. Many a mother, too, has gone out to work, either to augment her husband's earnings or, if she is widowed or otherwise alone, to provide enough for her child's skating needs.

This is a remarkable form of indirect devotion to the sport, especially when one considers that few think seriously at the time in terms of recovering the costs by turning professional. That kind of decision is not usually made until late in an amateur's career. Some of the top competitors eventually join ice shows, others become coaches, but a surprising number do neither, and the high cost of their training is never recouped.

There are people who watch top amateurs giving exhibitions in front of huge crowds, which sometimes exceed ten thousand, and jump to the conclusion that the skater is getting a cut from the proceeds. This is decidedly not the case. The ISU enforces strict regulations of amateurism, forbidding monetary recompense and limiting the value of prizes. No amateur skater is even allowed to perform exhibitions without written permission from the ISU or the relevant national association. Any box-office profits above the promotional costs go, more often than not, either to administrative funds formed to pay skaters' competition expenses, or to charity.

Generally speaking, there is no truer amateur in sport than the figure skater, though we all know of certain countries which heavily subsidize their

John Curry (left), followed his 1976 triple crown success — world, Olympic and European titles for Britain in one season — with a new approach to theatrical skating. Turning professional to develop his own ideas in the 'John Curry Theatre of Skating,' he was soon starring on the stage of the London Palladium with a classical ballet style not previously attempted on skates.

national sports training system and render a standardized worldwide enforcement of true amateurism quite impracticable. The inequality of costs and facilities is a fact of life and not the concern of this book, but, in whatever country and under whatever system, there is no doubt that skaters in training thoroughly enjoy themselves. Regardless of any pressure to win, the true pleasure of performing is self-evident. It is the sheer elegance of the sport which fascinates, the challenge to produce in three dimension what a painter strives to achieve on canvas.

Planning the pattern of a free skating programme is really an art within an art. The skater with a keen sense of showmanship must have an advantage. It is sensible first to think of a strong start and an impressive finish. A really attractive jump, perhaps a double axel, near the beginning serves a twofold purpose. It causes judges and audiences to sit up and take notice, to concentrate with greater interest, and it means attempting a difficult move while physically fresh.

The final item has to be enacted while tiring. It also has to end the display neatly, coming to a halt usually near the centre of the rink. A spin of some sort is a natural, popular choice, and a fast, cross-foot spin can be hardly bettered. A sit spin is also very suitable, but whether ending with or without a spin, coming finally to a full stop with a dramatic pose is what the crowd likes and signals instinctive applause.

The best of the other highlights need to be spread out intelligently through the four or five minutes in such a way that jumps, spins and spirals are suitably blended and separated at appropriate intervals. The audience wants to be kept interested throughout, but the competitor has to consider pacing the programme to suit stamina. Energetic leaps and gyrations need to be shrewdly interspersed with less fatiguing, but still pleasing, spirals and intricate footwork that can hold the attention.

The wise performer will arrange highlights in different parts of the rink, covering all areas in turn to provide an agreeable, symmetrical effect. Certain movements, like a split jump, are best done near the centre. Others, like a spreadeagle, may look better at one end. A sit spin too near the barrier will be lost from view for some. All such factors have to be carefully considered. But care has to be taken not to try anything difficult too near the barrier, allowing sufficient margin for any error that could otherwise cause an unnecessary crash. It is also prudent to cash in on the element of surprise, to keep the spectators wondering what is to follow by being unconventional. Originality pays. That is the way to retain interest, to avoid advertising, so far as is possible, what is coming next.

So an approximate order of technical content is conceived in the skater's mind. But it all has to be timed to music; free skating is for those born with a musical ear. One is no more likely to pursue this sport at a high level without being so gifted, any more than one would persevere too seriously with a musical instrument. However, given a good ear for music, selecting the most suitable accompaniment to the contents planned must be one of a free skater's greatest delights. Basically, it is a question of listening to lots of pieces until one discovers those with a pronounced beat at intervals ideal for the skating highlights proposed. To see and hear a skater timing each landing precisely to a dramatic beat of music is a real pleasure. This is a talent which some of the best technical skaters lamentably lack. Obviously, the skater with a keen sense of rhythm has a head start. With taping so easy nowadays, most opt for merging several pieces of music so that the best dramatic effect from each can be gained in one performance.

Those who instinctively ally the waltz to skating may be surprised to know that ideal accompaniment ranges from classical to pop, from film themes to disco and jazz. The scope is infinite. It gets to the stage where a skater listens to any and every item of music within earshot, consciously or not, to assess its skating potential — as this writer can testify.

I once embarked on a most fascinating adventure, to produce and compère a series of radio programmes which comprised interviews with famous skaters and recordings of the music with which their performances had become particularly associated. I can recall selections varying from Saint-Saëns' *The Swan* and Gounod's ballet music from *Faust*, to the contrasting rhythmic tempos of *In the Mood* and *Sabre Dance*. More recently, I devised two long-play records of some of the music most familiar to championship audiences. Some memorable world championship moments are recalled in these selections of music that has been brilliantly interpreted by celebrated ice stars. Included are the five-minute programmes used by Robin Cousins and Charlie Tickner in their respective championship performances. Cousins is a master in the art of choosing exactly what suits his skating best and one of his greatest successes was the catchy theme from the film, *The Railway Children*, which perfectly matched his incredibly fast sequence of intricate footwork timed to it.

The *Light Cavalry* overture by Franz von Suppé and the 'Torreador March' from George Bizet's *Carmen* are two of the most frequently chosen pieces by leading male free skaters because of their evocations of masculine virility and superb percussion accompaniment for jumps. Don Jackson is particularly associated with the strident *Carmen* music. In marked contrast, George Gershwin's *Rhapsody in Blue* has appealed to prominent women performers, notably Britain's Daphne Walker, and the Czechoslovak, Hana Maskova. Ever since it was used by Cecilia Colledge, *Dream of Olwen* by Vaughan Williams has also been considered especially suited to women skaters with ballet-style elegance.

Charles Tickner, the American who won the 1978 world title after the closest imaginable finish — nearly a triple tie, with Jan Hoffmann, the East German runner-up, and Robin Cousins, the third placed Briton. Charlie has been a powerful jumper whose earlier sound figures often gave him a useful final edge over his rivals.

Mikis Theodorakis's 'Zorba's Dance' from the film, *Zorba the Greek*, reminds ice-dancing fans of Bernard Ford and Diane Towler, Britain's four-time world champions, who interpreted this exotic melody so well. Characteristic ice-dance accompaniment to correct tango tempo is well reflected in a medley consisting of Victor Sylvester's *Golden Tango*, constantly used in ice-dance competitions, *Hernando's Hideaway* by Richard Adler and Jerry Ross, popularized by the Canadian ice dancers, David Porter and Barbara Berezowski, and Jacob Gade's *Jealousy*, interpreted so well by the Russians, Aleksandr Gorshkov and Ludmila Pakhomova.

Blockbuster musical-show selections are among championship skaters' favourites, so many being ideally descriptive and having the added advantage of appealing readily to audiences. Ernest Gold's theme from the film, *Exodus*, opens and closes with drum-roll highlights just made for jumps and spins, the whole punctuated with varied tempos conducive to graceful, balletic artistry.

The theme from the Normandy invasion film, *The Longest Day*, was skilfully interpreted by the United States ice dancers, Andrew Stroukoff and Susan Kelley, played in kilian tempo — a lively, marching rhythm. A selection from the very American music of Leonard Bernstein's *West Side Story* was surprisingly used in Tokyo by the 1977 Soviet World Ice Dance Champions, Andrei Minenkov and Irina Moiseeva, better known as 'Min and Mo'.

The Canadian, Ron Shaver, and the East German, Christine Errath, are among many who have capitalized on another film selection, from Jerry Bock's *Fiddler on the Roof*. Andrew Lloyd-Webber's score for *Jesus Christ Superstar* has proved very apt for many skaters, among them the Finnish Pekka Leskinen, and the American, Terry Kubicka. The United States pair skaters, Michael Botticelli and Sheryl Franks, used to great advantage Aram Khachaturyan's entrancing ballet suite, *Spartacus*, better known by some as the theme music used for the BBC television series, *The Onedin Line*.

It is one thing to seek guidance and opinion from one's coach or friends, both on the technical and musical content of a skating programme, but, in the main, if the skater does not largely create from personal ideas, the final result will not reflect the individual self-expression necessary to avoid seeming like someone else's creation. The truly innovative succeed in free skating. If a performer merely copies and repeats movements arranged by someone else, such as an instructor, it is not the skater whom the audience is seeing, but some other influence. The expert can even recognize a particular coach's characteristics, and knows that when several skaters skate in a similar way, they have probably been coached by the same person.

The televiewer may be mystified when hearing references to the 'short free' and the 'long free' programmes. To avoid any possible confusion, the long free is the final performance of a championship (five minutes for men, four for women), which is seen more frequently on the small screen. This is the *pièce de résistance*, in which each skater does exactly what he or she likes, as has been described, and it is worth fifty per cent of the total marks in a competition. The compulsory figures get thirty per cent and the remaining twenty per cent is earned in the middle section of a championship, the short free.

In this, each skater is required to perform, and suitably link, seven specified movements, announced before the season begins. The seven have to be performed within a maximum period of two minutes and to music of each skater's choice. Six of the elements required are usually two separate, named double jumps; a specified jump-spin combination; a named spin; a spin combination (i.e. with certain change-of-foot variations); and a

Christine Errath, the robust, always confident-looking East German whose personality appeal was so often enhanced by clever positioning of arms and hands, as seen here. World champion in 1974 and Olympic bronze medallist two years later, Christine had a way of standing with hands on hips after a performance, looking at the judges as if challenging them to give her high marks.

particular kind of footwork sequence. The other element is the most interesting, the one which often makes or breaks a competitor's overall chances. It is a two-jump combination consisting of a named double jump together with any double or triple jump of the skater's own choice. This option usually obliges male title contenders to include a triple, to gain precious extra marks, but fewer women take the risk.

The great point about the short free is that a skater is more heavily penalized for not correctly performing an element than when making a similar error in the long free. The judges are there to observe seven obligatory movements and, as in any kind of examination, failure in any one of them must entail a forfeiture of marks. Thus it is always a matter of great interest, particularly in the men's event, to know which optional multiple jump a skater elects to include in the jump combination.

In the long free skating, and to a lesser extent in the short free, the judges' task is far more comprehensive than merely adding marks for movements well accomplished, or docking marks for technical faults. They have to assess the variation of contents, degree of difficulty and manner of execution. They note whether speed is gathered without visible effort, and look for well-mixed original footwork on toes and edges, smooth transitions and changes in tempo, sudden surprise movements, good positioning with toes pointed and suitable posture, intelligent use of the ice area, choice of music and manner of its interpretation.

As general guidance for judges, the ISU broadly categorizes the main division of marks as follows: 0 = not skated; 1 = bad; 2 = unsatisfactory; 3 = mediocre; 4 = good; 5 = very good; and 6 = faultless.

Note that last word — faultless. A disturbing trend in championships during the last decade has been an almost casual and demeaning use of the maximum six mark. This revered score is cherished because it implies perfection, or should do, but it becomes farcical if awarded to a skater who makes a blatant error — and there have been too many instances of this. I recall when Janet Lynn, of the United States, fell heavily from a jump-sit spin during the 1972 Sapporo Olympics, yet still received a six from one judge for artistic merit. I did not think she fell all that artistically.

At the 1973 European Championships in Cologne, two Russians, Aleksandr Zaitsev and Irina Rodnina, received no fewer than twelve sixes, quite unprecedented, yet they made three palpable errors. When questioned on such a matter, the judge's stock reply is that, because someone earlier had received five-point-nine, a better performance had to be so acknowledged. My stock answer is that the average marks given for free skating are far too high, without allowing sufficient margins to play with, five-point-eight being commonplace at international championships. This is the more noticeable because the best figure traced rarely gets more than four-point-five, and that devalues compulsory figures.

Whenever asked about the most artistic solo skaters seen, four spring immediately to mind — Peggy Fleming, John Curry, Toller Cranston and Robin Cousins — and all have possessed a compulsive urge to approach perfection which absorbed them enough to make medals seem almost a secondary consideration. Each wished to elevate the sport to a fine art. To them, it was not enough to accomplish the most difficult jumps, spins, spirals and linking footwork. It was important that they performed them with style and finesse in a manner of detail to which only the very creative can aspire. In each case, this attitude was also reflected in non-skating interests.

A piano concerto greeted my ears one March morning in 1967, as I walked into the palatial main lounge of the Vienna Intercontinental Hotel.

Always a perfectionist at heart, Robin Cousins is motivated by sheer dedication of purpose, resolving to link the best jumps and spins into a carefully moulded presentation designed to appeal to spectators and judges alike.

Toller Cranston, the Canadian with a highly individualistic, innovative style, reached his amateur peak with an Olympic bronze medal at Innsbruck in 1976. Afterwards, like Curry but with a different approach, he formed his own touring ice show.

Looking instinctively for the loudspeaker from which the sound seemed to be coming, I saw instead, in an alcove half-hidden by a pillar, that the pianist was in fact in the room. Unaware of my presence, she continued as I marvelled at the considerable talent which this modest young lady until then had kept so secret. It was Peggy Fleming, and as soon as she saw me she stopped playing, shyly self-conscious and embarrassed at the discovery until I begged her to continue.

This was the frail-built, retiring girl who looked anything but an athlete, let alone the world's best woman skater in a sport demanding so much physical stamina and determination. She was very quiet-spoken and certainly *looked* more like a pianist than a skater, but appearances can be deceptive. This petite, brown-haired, blue-eyed American had another off-the-ice interest, ballet, and that was very easy to understand when watching her graceful hand and arm movements and high standard of choreographic presentation in her championship-winning programmes. Rapt in extreme concentration, she free skated with the same studious expression as when tracing figures.

On the rigours of competition, Peggy confessed: 'Of course it taxed my strength and time, but that was the challenge — to maintain a normal life along with the demands of training. There were lots of disappointments. Sometimes I fought against being human. But in overcoming these problems I learned, and that is what has made my skating life worthwhile.'

The unique style of John Curry reached its championship peak at the

1976 Innsbruck Olympics, when victory fulfilled an ambition for which he had striven with earnest dedication for more than a decade. He, too, gained inspiration from ballet. An Olympic gold medal, he believed, could become tangible evidence that he had achieved a target in the kind of self-expression which concerned him most. With the majestic finesse which nobody has succeeded in imitating, each of his deliberate and unhurried movements was perfectly paced. His three triple jumps — loops, salchow and toe loop — were never allowed to upset the rhythmic continuity of an elegant, shrewdly devised programme perfectly timed to ideally chosen music from *Don Quixote*.

John had always been a perfectionist. He once told me that titles, though great to have, were, to him, of secondary importance to personal improvement in technique. The latter he attained to such a high degree that some believed he had opened a new era of artistic skating. Compared with the traditional athleticism of most of his opponents, he developed an emphasis on a ballet-style grace, without neglecting or detracting from the difficult jumps, spins and linking spirals he so skilfully wove into a style entirely his own.

'I never even thought about it as a sport,' John insists. 'Skating is a very beautiful form of movement which I think has a great potential. On the ice we can move in a way that no one else can. It's not ballet, it's a form entirely in its own right.'

Toller Cranston, the tall Canadian with an exceptionally dramatic style, has displayed a less gentle, more dynamic approach. He, too, strove to change a sport into an art and, after gaining an Olympic bronze medal in 1976, turned professional before reaching his competition peak to cash in on his unusual theatrical impact. Many appreciate his innovative élan and interpretative actions. A man of many parts, he is also the author of several books and an accomplished painter and lithographer. Whenever trying to compare Toller with John, one realizes that with their greatly differing styles, one or the other will appeal according to individual preference, but both have shared that elusive objective, to develop skating to ever higher standards.

Robin Cousins has seemed always more down-to-earth in his manner of approach. First proclaimed the world's best free skater in 1978 when only twenty — eight years younger than when Curry reached that zenith — Robin would have been overall champion by then but for inconsistent figures. His repertoire of jumps and spins has exceeded those of his predecessors. Nobody before had jumped higher and with less fear, nor landed with such consistent precision on a true edge. His spins have been faster and more varied than those of any other championship contestant, past or present. His linking footwork has left nothing to be desired, with an overall manner of execution riveting the crowd's attention.

Therein lies one clue to the worldwide Cousins appeal. He always studied audience reaction. He has been conscious of intentionally commanding the spectators' attention right from the opening bars of his music, sustaining it throughout, and giving a better performance through the inspiration of their rapport. 'It is important to make sure that everybody is focussed on you,' he maintained, and he succeeded in making it so. Off the ice, he has spent much leisure time painting original cartoon characters, and could have become prominent in commercial art had he so preferred.

'To me,' says Robin, 'skating is being able to get on to the ice and express my feelings to an audience through music and the movements that make up skating. I don't think you can differentiate between skating being a sport or an art, because the idea is to make the sport like an art.'

Switzerland's Denise Biellmann, one of the most accomplished free skaters, whose overall success has been handicapped by comparatively weak figures. Nobody else can perform so well this grab-hold spin which she made a unique speciality, because every other girl competing against her found it physically impossible to hold a skate so high above her head while spinning.

Pair Skating

With a skillful one-handed grip, Aleksandr Zaitsev holds aloft his Russian partner, Irina Rodnina, as if she were a feather-weight, but Irina's long experience of technique enables her to make such a move as easy as possible for 'Sasha'. Irina won ten straight world pair skating titles, six with husband Zaitsev and four with her previous partner, Alexsei Ulanov, before taking time off to have a baby.

Why is it that an average of only seven nations have been represented in recent world pair skating championships, when the men's and women's singles at the same meetings have been contested by skaters from more than twenty countries? The figures reflect a diminishing participation at all levels in this event, in marked contrast with ever-increasing numbers of ice dancers.

It is surprising that, in view of the keen competition among soloists, more young skaters do not take the view that, because of the numerically weaker opposition, their chances of making international progress in pair skating are accordingly much greater. The physical demands, admittedly, are higher than those in ice dancing, but otherwise championship aspirants in either of the four events — men, women, pairs and ice dance — must devote a similar amount of time to training.

Because the number of pair contestants has grown smaller, the task of finding an experienced partner is correspondingly more difficult, but that need not deter any two young skaters starting together from scratch. A Soviet and East German dominance in the event is said to frighten others off, but that should be seen as a challenge, and the Americans, Randy Gardner and Tai Babilonia, set what ought to be an inspiring example in that respect by magnificently halting, in 1979, a fourteen-years' Russian run of world victories.

There are no compulsory figures in a pairs championship. The contest comprises just two sections — short and long programmes, corresponding in conception to those of solo free skating. In the short free, each pair is required to skate and suitably connect six obligatory elements, announced before the season begins, within a period of not more than two minutes and to music of the contestants' choice. Connecting steps are expected to be kept to a minimum and no extra marks are given if the performance is extended to the maximum time allowed if this proves unnecessary. Indeed, marks can be deducted if unprescribed elements are included.

The marks for the short free are worth a quarter of the total, the other three-quarters going to the long free, wherein each pair creates its own five-minute programme of technical contents and music. As in solo skating, a margin of ten seconds is allowed either way of the stipulated time, beyond which transgressors could be penalized for misjudgement.

Again, as in solo skating, two sets of marks (up to a six maximum) are awarded for each of the short and long programmes. In the first set of marks, for technical merit, the judges must consider difficulty, variety, cleanness and sureness. In the second set, for artistic impression, they have to assess harmonious composition of the programme as a whole and its integration with the music chosen; utilization of the area; easy movement and sureness in time to the music; carriage; originality; and expression of the character of the music.

Pair skating consists fundamentally of some movements while the partners are in bodily contact, and other movements while they are separated. The latter are termed shadow or mirror skating. The object throughout is to peform in harmony. When separated, they are not obliged always to perform the same movements as each other, but are expected at all

times to give an impression of unison — officially termed homogenous impression. What each does while separated is, naturally, no more than what a soloist can do, but linked together the two can perform a wide variety of lifts, spirals and throws which are possible only in pair skating and thus, for the onlooker, provide an attractive variation to single skating.

The only restrictions imposed are in the interests of safety and intended to curb any unnecessary display of muscular strength more suited to the circus ring. For example, in a lift the raised partner must be in a continuously ascending and descending rotational movement and not be held aloft in sustained pose. In all lifts, the partners may give each other assistance only through hand-to-hand, hand-to-arm and hand-to-body grips. Assistance by holding the legs is forbidden, neither is it permissible in a lift to turn a partner in horizontal positions — the kind of thing sometimes seen in a skating act on the variety stage.

The carrying partner may not execute more than three revolutions during one lift. Spinning movements in which the man swings the girl around in the air while holding her hand or foot are not allowed, nor is the jumping of one partner towards the other. Forbidden also are rotational movements with the grip of one of the partners on the leg, arm and neck of the other partner. All these are commonsense precautions, not only for safety, but to ensure that the character of the performance is acceptable. There are still plenty of exciting, daring manoeuvres which are permissible, some even sufficiently hazardous to increase the chances of injury during training.

The death spiral is characterized by the girl spiralling on one skate in circular motion round her partner, who acts as pivot, retaining virtually the same pose while holding her with one or both hands. For the man, controlled wrist and arm strength is a key factor. The girl may spiral in a

Soviet masters of the death spiral, Oleg Protopopov and his wife, Ludmila Belousova, perform the movement, in classically graceful style, for which they became most famous. The Protopopovs won four consecutive world titles in the sixties and, in 1968, successfully defended the Olympic crowns they had gained four years previously.

51

forward or backward direction on either edge of either blade, usually leaning well back until the rear of her head is in close proximity to the ice — hence the name death spiral. Outstanding performers who did much to further the popularity of this move were the West Germans, Hans-Jürgen Bäumler and Marika Kilius. Marika's blonde hair was always neatly groomed in an upswept style, and they were able to time the action so that her hair would literally sweep the ice enough for her to rise with snowy flakes still clinging to her hair.

The Russian married pair — Oleg Protopopov and Ludmila Belousova — who succeeded them as World Champions in 1965, appeared to be influenced by the West Germans in this move. And they even improved on the movement with added ballet-style grace, Ludmila excelling with particularly acute-angled edges. In fact, the Protopopovs introduced a smooth, slow elegance to much of their repertoire — too slow by today's standards — achieving a classical style reflecting the national love for ballet which they succeeded in transposing to the ice. At early morning outdoor practice during the 1968 Grenoble Olympics, I frequently found Audrey Hepburn, the film star, sitting alone on a rinkside bench, transfixed by their work-outs. An expert dancer, she confessed an obsessive admiration for the Protopopovs, who, she believed, introduced a refreshingly original dimension to pair-skating artistry.

Light and shadow stress the artistic effect of the West German pair skaters, Hans-Jürgen Bäumler and Marika Kilius, pictured on outdoor ice at Davos, Switzerland. Twice world champions, they defeated the Protopopovs with the best performance of their career within weeks of the Russians winning the Olympic title in 1964.

The couple successfully defended their Olympic title in Grenoble that year, but the most thrilling pairs contest I ever watched was when they were defeated by a whisker in the World Championships of 1964 in Dortmund, West Germany. Skating earlier than their main rivals, Bäumler and Kilius, their performance was very highly marked, and was adequate, it seemed, to ensure victory. The host nation's contenders followed with the knowledge that they needed sixes to win. Their task seemed impossible, but the Germans pulled out all the stops, risking everything in sheer desperation — and, remarkably, everything worked. I recall Marika wobbling dangerously after landing in backward direction from one lift. It appeared she must fall, yet somehow she retained equilibrium to avert a crash which assuredly would have deprived the home country pair of what proved to be the narrowest victory imaginable.

In the commonest form of pair sit spin, the partners face each other, the man holding the girl's waist while her hands are stretched wide on either side. With toes of their skating blades fairly close, they each spin while in sitting posture, so that the knee of the girl's skating leg is between her partner's lower thighs. As they spin, the girl's free leg is extended behind and the man's is extended in front. This move has been exquisitely performed by the Americans, Randy Gardner and Tai Babilonia, whose quickfire style makes their every action technically admirable, further enhanced by an instinctive theatrical flair. They also excel in the catch-waist camel spin, wherein partners gyrate in camel (arabesque) position, with bodies close together, each with an arm round the other's waist and with free legs pointing in opposite directions.

Among the best known pairs lifts currently popular in championships are the loop lift, overhead axel lift, lasso lift, split lutz lift and twist lift.

The partners approach the loop lift skating one behind the other, in hand-to-hand position. The girl, skating in backward direction on an outside edge, is lifted in a complete loop jump, with legs in split position or stretched. The man turns with his partner and lands her on the same backward outside edge.

In the most usual form of overhead axel lift — invented by the German, Ernst Baier — the movement begins with partners travelling forward in a hand-in-hand position. The girl is lifted from an outside forward edge and rotated one-and-a-half times above and to the rear of her partner's head, supported by his hand under her armpit. She lands on the back outside edge of the opposite blade to that used in take-off. The man rotates beneath his partner throughout the lift. The action is typified by a hand-to-hand full arm extension when the jump is at its peak.

The lasso lift is begun from a side-by-side, hand-to-hand approach, from which the girl is lifted from a forward outside edge. She rotates one-and-a-half times in split position, while her partner's outstretched arm is in a pose simulating that considered natural for lassoing a steer. A backward landing is effected on a right outside edge.

The split lutz lift commences with partners travelling backwards in side-by-side position. The girl is lifted from a back outside edge, making a lutz jump in the air, to land again on a back outside edge.

The twist lift has the accent on the girl's rotational movement during almost vertical descent before landing on a true edge. Generally speaking, the best exponents of lifts have been the great Irina Rodnina with her second partner and husband. Aleksandr 'Sasha' Zaitsev. Irina's timing has been masterly and her deep-edged control so precise, making many of their movements look deceptively easy. The powerful calf muscles, all-round strength and immense stamina of this sturdily built Russian, added to her

Randy Gardner and Tai Babilonia, the Americans who, in 1979 in Vienna, ended a fourteen years' Soviet monopoly of the world pairs title. Always exciting and more theatrical than most to watch, they are highly creative and have introduced a number of new sequences which others have failed to match in quality.

skating expertise, promoted a supreme confidence evident in her every action. Heralding each highlight with a characteristic sweep of an arm, she taught Sasha how to synchronize their solo spins and jumps in masterly fashion, and for years they had no peers in lift technique.

At their peak they were so good that on one occasion they continued their five-minute world-championship performance after their music had stopped through a technical fault, with more than two minutes left. Each of the nine judges awarded them five-point-nine for technical merit. It happened at Bratislava in 1973, an occurrence believed to be without precedent and unlikely to be repeated. The referee, in my view, was wrong in allowing them to go on and should have ordered a re-skate. How could any judge fairly assess musical interpretation to non-existent music? But there is no denying that the quality of their skating that day was extremely high.

Sasha and Irina perfected the triple twist lift to a fine art. Ironically, their compatriots, Sergei Shakrai and Marina Cherkasova, whose visual impact was aided by an abnormal height discrepancy, outdid their national champions with the first quadruple twist lift, at the 1977 European Championships in Helsinki.

Fairly recently developed pair movements have been the throw axel and the throw salchow, spectacular to watch because these moves involve the girl being thrown through the air from the force of her partner's axel or salchow jump, but she must land on the true edge of one blade to complete

The long and short of it — Sergei Shakrai and Marina Cherkasova, Soviet world runners-up in 1979, made a sensational international debut when Marina was only 13 and more than a foot shorter than her partner. This abnormal height discrepancy enabled them to become the first pair to accomplish a quadruple twist lift. Later, they also became the first to perform simultaneous triple jumps.

the movement correctly. Some top pairs, notably Zaitsev with Rodnina and Gardner with Babilonia, have developed these moves to involve triple jumps — hence a triple-throw axel or a triple-throw salchow. Teamwork, also, is the essence of pair skating. Partners need to be of technical standard either equal to, or suitably complementary to, each other. The man should be physically strong enough to lift his partner comfortably and the girl should be light enough to minimize her partner's lifting efforts. Inevitably, they will spend a large amount of their time in each other's company, so compatibility both on and off the ice should prove a considerable advantage if not an essential requirement.

The man ought to be the taller. A difference of three inches is ideal, though, of course, one cannot be sure whether a young team who start and stay together will grow in proportion. A few couples have capitalized on an extreme height difference. A good example was the American brother and sister, Ronald and Cynthia Kauffman, three times world bronze medallists during the 1960s. They were able to develop the Kauffman spin, since copied, in which he swung his leg over her head while both were gyrating. They used their contrasting heights intelligently and never looked comical. The Shakrai-Cherkasova team, when Marina was in her early teens and well over a foot shorter than Sergei, were able to accomplish some feats which their rivals could not match, but their efforts at that time were regarded more as a freakish novelty, likened to a puppet on a string, with too much emphasis on the man's physical strength.

Not only in pairs, but in all four figure skating events, the system of calculating results is one of the most complicated and perplexing in international sport. Each skater ends a championship with a total number of points and placements (ordinals). The points are the aggregate of marks gained from all nine judges, factorized where necessary to comply with the required percentages for each section of the competition. The placements figure is that reached by adding together the final positions of each of the nine judges given to a competitor.

But, contrary to what spectators might reasonably suppose, the winner is not necessarily the one with the highest number of points, nor the one with the lowest number of placements. These two totals offer no more than fairly good guidance to a skater's adjudged merit. The final overall positions are decided by what is known as the majority placing system. Under this method, the participant adjudged winner is the one with a *majority* of firsts (irrespective of total placements and total points). If an entrant has at least five firsts, that is it. If nobody has five firsts, the entrant having the most firsts with seconds is the winner, and so on down the list.

A quick way of illustrating this is to quote an example of one of the closest finishes I can recall, in the men's European championship of 1979 in Zagreb, when the nine judges placed the top three as follows.

Brother and sister John and Jennifer Nicks, who in 1953 became Britain's world pair champions. John has since enjoyed a distinguished career as coach in Los Angeles, his most successful pupils being the Americans, Randy Gardner and Tai Babilonia.

Judge No:	1	2	3	4	5	6	7	8	9	Total Placements	Total Points
Hoffmann	3	1	3	1	1	2	1	4	2	18	184.04
Kovalev	1	2	2	3	2	1	2	3	4	20	183.98
Cousins	2	3	1	2	3	3	3	1	1	19	184.54

Cousins had the most points, but did not win. He had the second lowest placements, but did not come second. A skater with a majority of first, i.e. five or more, would have won automatically, but because neither had that many, these three had to be assessed on collective majorities of firsts and seconds.

Aleksandr Zaitsev and Irina Rodnina go into a death spiral. Normally, the man is the guiding factor in a pair, but the outstanding Irina has been the undoubted master of this team — having carefully improved husband 'Sasha' after leaving her previous partner, Alexsei Ulanov. Irina's stamina has been incredible. Her acute-angled edges and sweeping arm actions characterize her performance.

For a member of the public to calculate such a result in advance of the official announcement, a degree in higher mathematics and a good computer may not be enough. The same system of judging operates for singles, pairs and ice dance events. And, fairest though this method of calculation may be, is it good for public relations? Does it help a sport if journalists and broadcasters need to explain such complicated statistics to their readers, listeners and viewers? In fact, the space or air time available is usually quite insufficient to do so and such explanations can well bore and confuse, anyway. I receive heavier mail on this one topic than on any other, every season.

An alternative system which I have suggested, and which met with approval from many experts when published in The *Daily Telegraph* in London and in the American magazine, *Skating,* in 1971, is to count and add together only the marks of the middle five judges for each participant (i.e. deleting the two highest and two lowest every time) — an idea successfully used in high diving and ski jumping. With a tenth judge also introduced on a rotational basis, so that no judge has to mark a compatriot, I believe such a system ought at least to be tried in lower-level competitions on an experimental basis. But, judging discrepancies, whether through incompetence or national bias, have been frequently evident in all four figure skating events. And the majority placings system is designed to offset any influence which erratic marking by one judge may have on a result.

The ISU in recent years has done much to minimize the chances of this happening, by adopting a firmer policy to suspend judges considered to be out of line. It is not uncommon for several judges at the end of a season to be suspended for a year or more. It is the referee of each event — the person who blows the whistle summoning the judges to display their marks — who recommends such suspension as and when deemed justified. In consequence, officials are wary of marking at great variance to their colleagues without being able to offer satisfactory reason.

In 1978, the ISU took the unprecedented step of suspending all Soviet officials for a season, a national penalty because of an accumulation of individual suspensions of that country's officials in preceding years. Without such safeguards, skaters obviously would not continue to compete if they felt they were not getting a square deal.

The three compulsory dances are selected each year from a schedule of twelve internationally recognized dances. The three, announced before the season starts to enable preparation, are those from either of the following groups:

1 Viennese waltz, Yankee polka, Blues.
2 Westminster waltz, Paso doble, Rhumba.
3 Starlight waltz, Kilian, Tango romantica.
4 Ravensburger waltz, Quickstep, Argentine tango.

For each of these compulsory dances, standardized music of suitable strict tempo is provided so that each couple skates to one of two pieces of music, the pieces played alternately to avoid monotony.

The original set-pattern dance allows a greater degree of freedom. Set-pattern means that certain steps of recognized design are skated on the same areas of the ice in repetitive sequences. The prescribed rhythm, made known before the season begins, might be either foxtrot, tango, polka, rhumba, march, waltz, samba or blues, and so on. Couples select their own music to accompany this and there is wide scope for originality of interpretation. Whereas the competitors' preceding compulsories inevitably resemble each other except in the skill of technical performance, each couple's effort in the set-pattern dance is distinctive.

Finally comes the free dancing — as much the event's highlight as is the free skating in the solo or pairs events. Each couple is free to devise a four-minute programme which, while retaining a recognizable dancing character, may include changes of tempo and of the type of dance, with originality encouraged, and all to a personal choice of music.

The competition is marked and factorized so that thirty per cent of the total score goes to the three compulsory dances (which each receive one set of marks, with six the maximum), a further twenty per cent goes to the original set-pattern dance, the remaining half of the total going to the free dance. The set-pattern and free dances each receive two sets of marks (up to six). The two sets for the set-pattern are for composition and presentation respectively. Those for the free dance are for technical merit and artistic impression.

Probably the four most commonly used technical terms in ice dancing, not normally occurring in the other events, are the chassé, choctaw, mohawk and twizzle. The chassé is a three-step sequence incurring a change of skating foot before the new skating blade passes the other. The choctaw is a turn involving a change of direction on to opposite edges of both blades (e.g. forward inside to backward outside). The mohawk is a half-turn, changing direction to similar edges (e.g. forward outside to backward outside). The twizzle is a very quick, counter-wise 180 degrees rotation of the blade, made virtually on one spot and from an outside edge.

The following is a brief resumé of the twelve standard dances now used in the compulsory section, including in parentheses their inventors, and when and where each was first performed.

The Viennese waltz (Eric Van der Weyden and Eva Keats, Streatham, London, 1934), is skated at a lively pace with strongly curved edges, using the conventional waltz hold throughout. The man holds his partner with the right hand firmly between her shoulder blades. Her left hand rests slightly below his right elbow. The man's left arm and his partner's right arm are extended to the side, with elbows slightly dropped and hands held normally a little above shoulder level.

The Yankee polka (James Sladky, Judy Schwomeyer and Ron Ludington, Wilmington, Delaware, 1969), is best described as a 'bouncy' dance,

David Porter and Barbara Berezowski, the most successful Canadian ice dancers in recent years, are one of the best-looking couples to be seen on the ice — David huskily handsome and Barbara elegantly beautiful. Their natural flair for showmanship prompted an early switch from the amateur ranks.

containing many short, precise steps, requiring partners to remain in close hold, particularly when turning rapidly around each other.

The Blues (Robert Dench and Lesley Turner, Streatham, London, 1934). With a slow tempo, this is skated with bold edges and offers plenty of scope for creative musical interpretation in 'slinky' night club mood.

The Westminster waltz (Eric Van der Weyden and Eva Keats, Westminster, London, 1938), features alternate waltz and kilian positions, the latter using a thumb pivot grip for the hands to facilitate the changing of sides by the partners. The girl's hands are held above her partner's, with the thumbs extended upwards into the man's fists.

The Paso doble (Reginald Wilkie and Daphne Wallis, Westminster, London, 1938), includes unusual two-footed slide steps, performed on the flat of the blades. The partners' relative positions change during the dance from outside (tango) to closed (waltz) to open (foxtrot).

The Rhumba (Walter Gregory, Westminster, London, 1938), skated throughout in kilian position, is typified by smooth hip movements of the skating leg and an emphasized side swing of the free foot.

The Starlight waltz (Courtney Jones and Peri Horne, Queen's Ice Club, London, 1963), is skated with the character and rhythm of the Viennese waltz, and is not a difficult dance. It is performed in waltz hold except for one brief change to kilian hold.

The Kilian (Karl Schreiter, Vienna, 1909). To march tempo, this dance tests close and accurate footwork, also unison of rotation and control. It is skated throughout in kilian position, with partners facing in the same direction, the girl on the man's right. With his right arm behind her back, their right hands are clasped, resting over the girl's right hip bone. The girl's left arm extends in front, across her partner's body, to hold his left hand.

The Tango romantica (Aleksandr Gorschkov, Ludmila Pakhomova and Elena Tschaikowskaja, Moscow, 1974), is the first international dance to be invented by Russians and expresses the interpretative characteristics of the tango. It needs to be skated on deep edges.

The Ravensburger waltz (Erich and Angelika Buck, Krefeld, West Germany, 1973). Skated as a Viennese waltz, with one brief change to kilian hold, this is an elegant, adventurous dance testing the skill of the twizzle turn.

The Quickstep (Reginald Wilkie and Daphne Wallis, Westminster, London, 1938). To fast music of bright character, this is danced throughout in kilian hold. The couple remain hip to hip, the man's right hip against his partner's left.

The Argentine tango (Reginald Wilkie and Daphne Wallis, Westminster, London, 1938). To tango tempo and in Latin-American style, this is a difficult dance requiring deep edges and appreciable élan. Strong flow and fast travel over the ice are essential.

The first ten world championships were won convincingly by British ice dancers, with compatriots as runners-up on five of those occasions and national grand slams on two of them. During that period, Lawrence Demmy and Jean Westwood, the first winners of the title, had four successive victories. Courtney Jones also won four times, twice with June Markham as partner and twice with Doreen Denny. Then came the first signs that the pupil was catching up with the master.

The run was broken by four straight successes by a Czechoslovak couple, Pavel Roman and Eva Romanova, before the title was recaptured for Britain and held for another four years by Bernard Ford and Diane Towler. Since their retirement in 1969, Russian couples have dominated the scene, notably Aleksandr Gorshkov and Ludmila Pakhomova, who achieved a

Aleksandr Gorshkov and Ludmila Pakhomova, the first Russians to become world ice dance champions, in 1970, went on to win it for a record six times in seven years. They won the first Olympic ice dance event, at Innsbruck in 1976. Regarded by many as the best exponents to date, they succeeded in their latter seasons to blend the best of eastern and western styles and together invented a new international dance, the tango romantica.

record number of six victories in seven years.

 Many consider Alek and Ludmila to have been the best ever, though some believe Bernard and Diane have had no peers. But preference depends so much on individual appreciation of style. Personal opinion counts more in this event. In solo or pair skating, jumps, spins or lifts are seen more clearly to be correct or faulty, but in ice dancing technical efficiency is a smaller part of the whole, style being a highly important factor. Yet who is to say always whether one style is right and another wrong? It is much more a question of individual taste.

 Bernard and Diane were the most versatile ice dancers, more adaptable and exceptionally good at fast tempo, their synchronization of free leg actions often approaching perfection. They epitomized the best of the British traditional technique. Alek and Ludmila were different. They introduced a more classical, smoother performance heavily influenced by Russian ballet. Both couples appealed in their own separate ways and, while it would be wrong, perhaps, to suggest that either pair was better than the other, it is certainly true that nobody else has yet quite attained the exceptionally high standards they set.

 The difference between free dancing and pair skating is much greater than the first-time spectator might suppose. Free dancing is, or should be, strictly limited to acceptable dance movements. The ISU rules state that the free dance shall consist of non-repetitive combinations of new or known dance movements composed into a programme which displays the personal ideas of the dancers in concept and arrangement.

The ice dance waltz hold (left) not unlike the conventional ballroom positions, is here demonstrated by Britain's Chris Dean and Jayne Torvill. The contrasting kilian side-by-side hold (right), is shown by the Hungarians, Andras Sallay and Kris Regöczy.

The free dance must be constructed so that the element of competitive dancing is predominant and so that the free dance shall not have the character of a pair skating programme. The competitors' general knowledge and ability in dancing, as well as the originality and concept of their ideas, are evaluated. Feats of strength and skating skill which do not form part of the dance sequence, but which are inserted to show physical prowess, are counted against the competitors using them. Certain free skating movements, such as turns, arabesques, pivots, etc., are permitted with the following limitations:

1 Separations of partners for steps, arabesques, pivots, etc., are permitted for not longer than five seconds. A separation during the final sequence of the dance is permitted for not longer than eight seconds.

2 Arabesques and pivots may not exceed the duration of the movements of the compulsory dances.

3 Pirouettes may not exceed three revolutions.

4 Skating on toe picks may not be done excessively.

5 Short jerky movements are acceptable only when they emphasize the character of the music.

6 Stops, in which couples remain stationary on the ice surface while performing body or twist movements or poses, may not exceed two measures of music.

7 Small dance lifts, in which the man may not raise his hands higher than his waistline, are permitted provided they fit the character of the music or emphasize certain passages of the music. These lifts may not have more than one-and-a-half revolutions.

Courtney Jones and Doreen Denny, twice British winners of the world ice dance championship. Courtney previously won twice with another partner, June Markham. Courtney later became chairman of the National Skating Association of Great Britain and Doreen was appointed coach at the prestigious Broadmoor Arena in Colorado Springs. With Peri Horne, Courtney devised the starlight waltz.

Pavel Roman and Eva Roman-ova, the superbly matched Czechoslovak brother and sister, ended nine years of British ice dance domination when they captured the world title in 1962. They held on to it for four years before Bernard Ford and Diane Towler regained it for the nation which largely pioneered this most elegant form of competitive skating.

8 Small low dance jumps, for the purpose of changing the foot or direction of one of the partners, are permitted provided that they do not exceed one-half of a revolution and that they are executed in dance position or at not more than two arms-length. Both partners may not jump at the same time.

These extracts from the ISU regulations stress the difference between the two kinds of skating in partnership. However, the following significant paragraph, from the ISU rule 512, was frequently disregarded by many leading couples during the 1970s:

A free dance programme which contains too many lifts, jumps, open [partners separated] and hand-in-hand positions, skating side by side, one after the other, or mirror-skating is more pair skating than free dancing and must be severely penalized by the judges.

As one member of the ISU Ice Dance Committee commented, the judges have always been capable of recognizing the breaches of rules, but have never had the courage to apply the appropriate penalties. It was because the spirit of the rules had been contravened so much, that the ISU in 1978 issued a statement which began:

The general principles of free dancing, and particularly rule 512, are not being observed nor adequately penalized by the judges. This oversight is allowing free dancing to develop into pair and show skating because the skaters and trainers, in the absence of penalization by the judges for disregard of the rules, assume that such disregard is permissible.

The statement continued with detailed guidance for judges, with a view to ensuring that the rules be observed *more* conscientiously in the future.

'The Olympics are what it's all about.' Such is the oft-expressed view of many star performers in skating and other sports. They gear their career training with a possible Olympic medal the most cherished goal, pacing themselves to reach their peak in an Olympic season. World titles, although officially regarded as more important, do not have quite the same magic or prestige.

This is probably because of the tremendous impact which the quadrennial Olympic celebrations have enjoyed, even before the days of television, garnering such wide publicity, from so many sources beyond the normal. I often describe the Winter Olympics as the greatest showcase for the sports concerned, the one and only occasion every four years when figure and speed skaters, ice-hockey players, alpine and nordic skiers, bobsledders and tobogganists all congregate as integral national teams, collectively housed and intermingling in social activities at one and the same specially constructed competitors' village.

These are golden opportunities to foster international goodwill. Earnest though the competition may be, the happiness and mutual respect shared by Olympic participants at mealtimes and during relaxed recreation between their big events assuredly promotes a truer understanding and realization of how similar we really all are, which cannot be a bad thing.

The Olympic début of figure skating was unique among ice and snow sports, being the first to gain such status. Sixteen years before the first separate Olympic Winter Games, figure skating was accepted as part of the 1908 Olympics in London, due largely to the centrally situated convenience of the indoor Prince's Skating Club rink in Knightsbridge. Narrow by present-day standards, the ice surface was two hundred feet long, but only fifty-two feet wide.

Ulrich Salchow, who has won more world men's titles than anyone else, was a fitting first winner, though only by a three to two judges' decision. Britain's Madge Syers, the outstanding woman skater of the period, not only won the individual gold, but, with her husband, Edgar, also gained a bronze in the pairs event won by the Germans, Heinrich Burger and Anna Hübler.

With figure skating thus under the critical microscope, the official report of the 1908 Olympic Games included this encouraging seal of approval:

> If control over the muscles, graceful movement, and a complete equilibrium of physical resources can ever be said to have been attained in the Olympic programme, it was to be seen in this competition; and the skating events should therefore take very high rank in any serious comparison between the various items in the Olympic Games of 1908 and previous years. The fact that these events call for not only strength but skill, both delicate and precise, not merely for natural ability but for patient and prolonged practice, and that these qualities can be exemplified by competitors of varying ages, of both sexes, and of many different nations, is a recommendation possessed by very few sports to a similar degree in the long catalogue of first-rate international championships.

The second Olympic figure skating competitions were included in the 1920 Games held in Antwerp, Belgium. Here, Gillis Grafström, creator of

Dorothy Hamill (right), was twice runner-up before winning the world title for the United States in 1976 at Gothenburg, Sweden, only a fortnight after taking the Olympic gold at Innsbruck. Her own style of camel jump-spin was dubbed the 'Hamill camel'.

the flying sit spin, succeeded his Swedish compatriot, Salchow, who, defending the men's title at the age of forty-two, still managed to finish fourth despite a leg injury. Theresa Weld became the first United States medallist. Although the best woman free skater, she ended overall third because of her weaker figure performance. Ice hockey made its Olympic début in Antwerp and, had it not been for skiing, the two sports on skates might well have continued in the regular Games schedule.

For the acceptance of nordic skiing led to the logical creation of a linked, but self-contained Winter Olympic Games, the first being staged in 1924, high in the French Alps at Chamonix. It was also the first outdoor Olympic skating, and a large amount of snow had to be cleared from the rink before the events began. Grafström attained his second gold, placed first by only four of the seven judges, to gain a narrow verdict over the rising Austrian, Willy Böckl. The much more comfortable women's victor was Herma Plank-Szabó, an Austrian who won five consecutive world titles. Last in a women's field of eight was an endearingly diminutive eleven-year-old Norwegian named Sonja Henie.

No fewer than three men and five women at that time doubled in solo and pair events. Andrée Joly, third with Pierre Brunet in the pairs, was also fifth for France among the women. The fourth placed British pair comprised John Page, fifth in the men's event, and Ethel Muckelt, who took the women's bronze. Such doubling is seldom attempted today, the training requirements to reach top level in any one event being too arduous to allow duplication.

Sonja Henie, pictured as a young Olympic champion, with skirt shorter than those of her rivals yet still long compared with those she later wore in her earliest films. From 1927 to 1936, she was never beaten in ten straight world and three consecutive Olympic contests.

The second Winter Olympics at St Moritz, the élite Swiss Alpine resort, in 1928, presented a master at his peak and a prodigy on her way up — the last of Grafström's three men's victories for Sweden, and the first of Sonja Henie's three women's wins for Norway. There was also the first of two pairs triumphs for Pierre Brunet and his future wife, Andrée Joly, of France. The spectators, although they could not know it at the time, were seeing at one meeting the two soloists whose record of three golds still stands — and the pairs winners whose achievement remains unbettered today.

The third Winter Olympics, and the first to be put on outside Europe, took place in 1932 at Lake Placid, New York. The easy second victory of Sonja, then at the zenith of her form, was well matched for interest in the men's event, with Grafström, at thirty-eight, attempting a fourth straight success. Karl Schäfer of Austria, at twenty-two almost a generation younger, gained a five-to-two verdict from the judges, and we shall never know whether the great Swede, a worthy runner-up, could possibly have pulled it off but for a nagging knee injury.

At the picturesque Bavarian resort of Garmisch-Partenkirchen, the 1936 Winter Olympics were organized on a scale not previously matched, with the host country intent on prestige. Whether the desired effect was attained is another matter. For the first time, Baron Pierre de Coubertin, founder of the modern Olympic series, excused himself from the opening ceremony, inevitably dominated by Hitler.

It was here that the promising Freddie Tomlins, who was to be killed in the war so soon after, made his only Olympic appearance for Britain. An example of his high-spirited impetuosity was recounted to me by his national rival and friend, Graham Sharp. Telling Graham he intended to get 'old Schickelgruber's autograph', Freddie proceeded by devious means to bore his way through Hitler's SS bodyguard, reputed to be impassable, and went up to the surprised dictator and gave him a pencil. He got the autograph but what the SS guards got afterwards was, I gather, less rewarding.

This aerial view of Lake Placid, venue for the 1980 Winter Olympics, shows the outdoor oval speed skating circuit on the right of the new $16 million Fieldhouse Ice Arena and, behind it, the 1932 Olympic Ice Arena used the second time around for training. In the foreground, beside the speed circuit, is Lake Placid High School, converted for the Games into a working Press Centre for 1,750 journalists. The stretch of water nearest the ice rink complex is Mirror Lake and the farther one is Lake Placid.

Sonja Henie, who became a legend in her own time, gained her final victory with much less to spare than at Lake Placid. The earlier wide gap between her rivals had decreased and Britain's Cecilia Colledge, who was to become world champion the following season, proved a formidable challenger. One judge placed the two girls equal and the Norwegian was probably wise to turn professional soon afterwards.

Karl Schäfer, a star pupil of the Vienna Skating School's most glorious era, retained without difficulty the men's crown he had captured from Grafström in 1932. This time, the Austrian's nearest challenger was Ernst Baier, who, with his future wife, Maxi Herber, was compensated by a hard-won victory for the host nation in the pairs contest. More experienced technique split the judges seven-to-two in the Germans' favour over their close rivals, a young Viennese brother and sister, Erich and Ilse Pausin. The Garmisch skating was a huge success but, alas, the omnipresent swastikas heralded the cessation of all Olympic sport for twelve years.

The fifth Winter Olympics were originally planned for 1940 at Sapporo, Japan, but war intervened and Sapporo had to wait another thirty-two years. The selection of St Moritz, the first venue to be host for a second time, was influenced by prevailing conditions when the Games were resumed in 1948. The Swiss resort's already existing facilities appealed, as did its geographical and political suitability. The mood throughout the programme appeared to be that of a brave front being put up by Europeans still suffering in many respects from the aftermath of battle, but the significant thing was that the Olympic flame could be re-kindled in spite of countless frustrations. The palpable will to revive the Games was heartening. Never did Baron de Coubertin's oft-quoted phrase, 'the importance of taking part', have a truer ring. Come what may, nations and individuals were determined to make a show in face of considerable problems, not least that of sadly inadequate funds for travel and accommodation.

While, in the interim, Europeans had marked time on skates, clearly the North Americans had not. The American, Dick Button, and the Canadian, Barbara Ann Scott, presented a first glimpse of the new transatlantic school of theatrical athleticism in jumps. Displaying physical strength and suppleness, Button was the forerunner of a revolutionary trend that was to characterize future men's free skating. And when Oslo played host in 1952, this great skater repeated his 1948 success, adding for good measure the first true triple jump to be achieved in Olympic competition, a triple loop. Superb figure tracings gained the women's gold medal for Britain's Jeannette Altwegg, even though she was surpassed in the free skating by the spectacular French girl, Jacqueline du Bief, and two Americans, Tenley Albright and Virginia Baxter. Jeannette's finest hour came, somehow appropriately, at a time when eyes were focussed more particularly on the British entrant for sadder reasons, spectators earlier having observed a minute's silence respecting the death of King George VI.

This was Jeannette's farewell competition appearance and, instead of following the vogue to capitalize in professional ranks, she won wide admiration by accepting a post at the Pestalozzi children's village at Trogen, Switzerland. Jeannette's indifference to publicity is typified by one occasion when Teddy Tinling, the tennis couturier, sought my co-operation to persuade her to model his new design for skating wear. Most girls would have jumped at the chance, but Jeannette, gracious as always, firmly declined.

A delightful setting for the seventh Winter Olympics in 1956 was the Italian resort of Cortina d'Ampezzo, overlooked by snow-clad granite peaks of the majestic Dolomite mountains. Profits from Italy's nationalized

Tenley Albright, of the United States, was twice world champion, in 1953 and 1955. She crowned a notable career with an Olympic victory in 1956 at Cortina d'Ampezzo, Italy.

football pools largely subsidized the newly built four-decker grandstands of the lavish, open-air ice stadium. The technical and spectacular highlight was undoubtedly the free skating of the men's dominant American trio, Hayes Jenkins, Ronnie Robertson and David Jenkins (Hayes's younger brother), who finished in that order. Hayes won by virtue of a slender margin in the figures and, although his free skating was excellent, the contents of his programme were not quite so ambitiously daring as those displayed by Robertson — a sensational, at times almost acrobatic free skater. Tenley Albright echoed the American zest for jumping with a delicately dramatic performance in seemingly effortless, graceful style, resisting a close challenge from her advancing compatriot, Carol Heiss.

As the first Winter Olympics to be internationally televised, worldwide publicity brought substantial long-term commercial benefits, to ice and snow sports, and to Italy and Cortina in particular. Such obvious 'frozen' assets ensured no shortage of applicants to stage subsequent Games.

The 1960 Squaw Valley Olympics in California are personally remembered as the 'showbiz' Games, from the moment I shook hands with three welcoming Red Indians at Reno airport and was introduced to Bruce Mapes, owner of Reno's fabulous Mapes Hotel. He insisted on my staying at his hotel, which positively bristled with show stars who seemed to take daily turns driving me to the rink. Sometimes it was Sammy Davis Jr and his manager, John Robinson, the latter a highly articulate man who quoted Sir Winston Churchill's wartime speeches verbatim during those forty-mile journeys. A seeming galaxy of other friendly stars included Mickey Rooney, looking just like Andy Hardy with a middle-aged spread, and Victor Borge, pronouncing his punctuation marks.

Gaby Seyfert, the first East German to win a world title, in 1969, successfully defending it the following season. Her sturdy, robust frame contrasted with the delicately petite American, Peggy Fleming, in whose shadow Gaby had to be content with three world silver medals and an Olympic silver. Each time she was bettered by her persistent US rival.

One morning, when hurrying from the chalet-style press centre, I nearly tripped over a girl squatting on the entrance steps. 'What a stupid place to sit!' I exclaimed, then realized I had thus addressed Jayne Mansfield, posing for a photographer as only she could. I did not know how to cover my embarrassment and she, bless her, had little to cover anything.

'The gamble which came off' is a phrase aptly describing the choice of Squaw Valley, the IOC having voted years earlier for an empty, then scarcely known site where everything had to be built from scratch. As pageantry chairman, Walt Disney supervised all the ceremonial arrangements and did not miss a trick. But the miracle of these Games was the weather. After weeks of rain, fresh snow and strong winds threatened to ruin the elaborately planned opening.

Then, with only fifteen minutes to go, as if by magic the clouds cleared, the sun shone and only the humourist attributed this dramatic effect to Disney. Throughout the entire eleven-day meeting, warm Californian sunshine on incongruous-looking snow and ice blessed the proceedings.

At the architectural prize-winning Blyth Arena, the American, David Jenkins, included high triple and double jumps of a standard which no European could match. His future sister-in-law, Carol Heiss, won the women's event by a comfortable margin and the Canadian combination, Robert Paul and Barbara Wagner, were equally convincing in the pairs.

A demonstration of strength from the powerful Oleg Proto-popov as he holds aloft his partner, Ludmila Belousova, during the Russian pair's prac-tice for a special ice gala before Queen Elizabeth the Queen Mother at London's Streatham rink in 1962. Oleg's and Lud-mila's second Olympic triumph in 1968 was a feat previously matched only by Pierre Brunet and Andrée Joly of France.

The closing ceremony was joyous, epitomizing the friendships made among competitors and spectators, yet tinged with a sadness born of the realization that all good things have to end. As the national anthem played and the flags were lowered, always an emotional moment, I had the honour of sharing that unforgettable experience with an incredibly beautiful Marlene Dietrich. My celebrated companion and I exchanged meaningful looks without words. There were tears in our eyes, which can be understood only by anyone who has personally attended Olympic pomp and circumstance.

At the commendably well organized 1964 Innsbruck Olympics, Queen Juliana of the Netherlands saw an inspired Sjoukje Dijkstra capture her country's first gold medal in any sport since the triumph of Fanny Blankers-Koen on the athletics track in 1948. Manfred Schnelldorfer took the men's title for West Germany. The pairs attracted more than usual interest when the classically smooth Soviet partnership, Oleg Protopopov and Ludmila Belousova, pipped the West German world title-holders, Hans-Jürgen Bäumler and Marika Kilius, in a thrillingly close tussle between the two best pairs to be seen for a long time. Protopopov's strength in lifts and his partner's acute-angled edges were rare sights for the connoisseur.

No fewer than five of the American team in Innsbruck were under sixteen, including Scotty Allen, the men's bronze medallist just two days before his fifteenth birthday, and Peggy Fleming, who finished sixth among the women. Such high placings among much more experienced opponents were agreeably more surprising than the reason for their presence. That tragic loss of an entire United States team in an air crash three years previously was still fresh in our memories.

But the youngest of all the competitors was a very small, slender-framed Czechoslovak boy, Ondrej Nepela, who had become thirteen only a month earlier. At the request of the women's page editor of the *Daily Telegraph*, I asked Ondrej and two of the other 'babes' in the Games if they felt nervous before venturing on to the vast ice expanse of a luxury stadium packed with eleven thousand intensely critical onlookers.

All answered emphatically in the negative, but it was Nepela's idol and mentor, Carol Divin, twice champion of Europe, who gave the most plausible answer to my enquiry. 'When they are so young, they have no fear,' he said. 'That is one reason why it is important for a would-be champion to start early. The older you become, the more you think. The more you think, the more you worry — and *then* you get nervous.'

The 1968 Grenoble Olympics provided a shock form upset when Emmerich Danzer, then world men's champion, lapsed in the figures and his fellow Austrian, Wolfgang Schwarz, took the title with dominant free skating. A fascinating feature of the women's free skating was the contrasting technique of the classical, frail-looking Peggy Fleming, the United States winner, and the robust East German, Gaby Seyfert, who came second. The outcome was hardly in doubt because of the American's substantial lead in the figures. Peggy's slender frame belied a remarkable stamina which sustained a widely varied repertoire of smoothly landed double jumps and graceful fast spins.

The retention of the pairs title by the Soviet husband-and-wife partnership, Oleg Protopopov and Ludmila Belousova, under which name she always skated, was a praiseworthy accomplishment at the ages of thirty-five and thirty-two respectively. But a long and successful career was obviously nearing its end and many people breathlessly admired their skilfully timed split lutz lift and characteristic one-handed death spiral.

Although skaters had separately represented East and West Germany in World Championships since 1956, they were required by the IOC to

At the age of ten, Ondrej Nepela idolized his Czechoslovak compatriot, Carol Divin, who came second in the world in 1962. 'One day I hope to be as good,' said the little boy and his ambition was more than realized when two second places followed three successive world titles from 1971 to 1973 — plus the Olympic gold medal in 1972 for good measure.

Sjoujke Dijkstra, the former Dutch triple champion, practising at Richmond Ice Rink in 1964, prior to appearing in 'Holiday on Ice'.

In typical ballet pose is Janet Lynn, who stole American hearts with a winning personality in the early seventies. But her friends boosted her so much that she wilted under the pressure of their expectancy. In the 1972 Olympics at Sapporo, Japan, the immaculate figures of the Austrian winner, Trixi Schuba, proved just too good, and so did Canadian runner-up Karen Magnussen, leaving the stout-hearted Janet with only a bronze. Victory also narrowly eluded her when beaten by Karen in the 1973 world championship.

compete in Olympic events as a unified German team until the 1968 Grenoble Games, when they skated for the first time under different banners.

At Sapporo, Japan's second largest city, the first Winter Olympics to be held in Asia was very efficiently staged in 1972. Ondrej Nepela, the youngest competitor at Innsbruck eight years previously, was now mature enough to become the first Czechoslovak to win an Olympic figure skating title. Sergei Chetverukhin's second place was the highest a Russian had achieved in a solo event.

Some of the best figures ever traced clinched the women's crown for the tall Austrian, Trixi Schuba, whose free skating was relatively moderate yet adequate for overall victory. There was an enthralling tussle for the silver between two much better free skaters, Karen Magnussen of Canada and Janet Lynn of the United States, the latter losing a close verdict.

That great Soviet pair skater, Irina Rodnina, with the earlier of her two partners, Alexsei Ulanov, gained a narrower decision than that to which she was becoming accustomed, by a six-to-three judges' margin over their Leningrad rivals, Andrei Suraikin and Ludmila Smirnova. The high quality of skating at Sapporo was memorable. Off the ice, I cannot forget the attractive female Japanese taxi driver who completely lost her way, enabling me to view some welcome oriental sights.

Owing to the late withdrawal of Denver, Colorado, as prospective host for the 1976 Winter Olympics, the IOC adopted a well justified 'better the devil you know' attitude by allocating the Games for a second time to Innsbruck. So two Olympic flames, one commemorating 1964, burned as warmly as the hearts of the hospitable Austrians.

As the competitors and officials paraded in the opening ceremony's traditional march past, the proud national flag bearer leading the British team proved an appropriate choice. It was John Curry, who was soon to become much better known. His glorious men's victory, the first-ever for Britain, involved a flawless final free-skating performance of majestic finesse. Each of his deliberate and unhurried movements was perfectly planned and the fascinated crowd sensed that, although his major rivals had yet to skate, none could overtake him. His three triple jumps were never allowed to upset the rhythmic continuity of an always elegant programme.

Neither Vladimir Kovalev, the Soviet runner-up, nor Toller Cranston, the Canadian bronze medallist, could match Curry's sterling display. Also among the vanquished were the reigning Soviet world champion, Sergei Volkov, and East Germany's 1974 World Champion, Jan Hoffmann. Earlier, tension had been heightened by unusually meticulous scrutiny of the figure tracings, several judges getting down on all fours to examine the turns, and when one even laid full-length on the ice it seemed that only a magnifying glass and deerstalker cap were missing from the Holmesian image.

Dorothy Hamill convincingly won the women's title, the third American to do so. The runner-up was Holland's California-based Dianne de Leeuw, who had defeated Dorothy in the 1975 World Championship. The pairs contest was won comfortably by the Soviet duo, Aleksandr Zaitsev and Irina Rodnina, the latter retaining the title she had gained at Sapporo with her previous partner, Alexsei Ulanov. Aleksandr Gorshkov and Ludmila Pakhomova became the first Olympic ice-dance champions. Nobody could deny the elegant Moscow couple their right to this historic honour, having by this time earned general recognition as the world's outstanding performers in this most graceful branch of figure skating.

The IOC selection of Lake Placid, as venue for 1980, and Sarajevo, Yugoslavia, for 1984, and also the strong support for the narrowly failing bid by Sapporo in the latter instance, were each significant portents concerning the likely sites for all future Winter Olympics. Officials with whom I have conferred now appear to believe that the most practical solution to the growing financial dilemmas of staging the Winter Olympics is to allocate the Games on a rotational basis to the four most suitable permanent centres possessing approved sites and accommodation.

There appears to be an approaching worldwide unanimity of thought regarding which four venues these should be — Innsbruck, Lake Placid, Sapporo and Sarajevo — with the latter subject to its success in 1984. These centres are geographically well spread, and Sarajevo has gained favour as what is now considered to be the most acceptable venue to represent Eastern Europe.

The growth of Olympic participation since 1908 is illustrated by the following table, which, as a separate breakdown of figure skating entries, is not believed to have been previously printed elsewhere.

Vladimir Kovalev, Soviet victor in 1977 and again in 1979, never appeared so versatile a jumper as his main rivals, but often gained by their errors. While others fell from difficult triples, Vladimir was content to accomplish lesser feats correctly and the tactics sometimes paid dividends. When forced to attempt the triples he least liked, the pressure proved too much and this cost him Olympic and world victories in 1976, when John Curry at his best just could not be matched.

Olympic Figure Skating Entries

Year	Venue	Nations	Men	Women	Pairs	Dance	Total*
1908	London	6	9	5	3	—	20
1920	Antwerp	8	9	6	8	—	31
1924	Chamonix	11	11	8	9	—	37
1928	St Moritz	12	17	20	13	—	63
1932	Lake Placid	13	12	15	7	—	41
1936	Garmisch	16	25	24	18	—	85
1948	St Moritz	12	16	25	15	—	71
1952	Oslo	15	14	25	13	—	65
1956	Cortina	15	16	21	11	—	59
1960	Squaw Valley	14	19	26	13	—	71
1964	Innsbruck	15	24	30	17	—	88
1968	Grenoble	17	28	32	18	—	96
1972	Sapporo	18	17	19	16	—	68
1976	Innsbruck	18	19	21	14	18	104
1980	Lake Placid	19	17	32	11	12	95

*This column does not take into account the relatively few instances when a competitor contested more than one event at the same meeting.

Theatre On Ice

There is certainly an element of the circus about today's professional touring ice revue. It visits each town on its itinerary not more than once a year, and everywhere its arrival is much heralded. The equipment and trappings, though very different to that of the circus, are correspondingly elaborate.

Instead of transporting and erecting a big top, it carries and instals a normal rink-sized ice tank which, like its attendant refrigerating power plant, is fully portable. It caters for a similarly large auditorium and, because of this, the accent is on the visually spectacular. Like the circus, too, it caters for the family audience, and even has its skating clowns. But there is something about an ice show which extends beyond the vast expanse of frozen stage, across the footlights and into the audience's hearts as they sit watching each wonder unfold, gripped by the essence of show-business flamboyance coupled with the excitement generated by sporting achievement. It sets out to appeal to all tastes and ages with a kaleidoscope of colour, elegant motion and emotion, thrills and spectacle.

A rightful claimant to be the first show skater of real consequence would be a German called Charlotte Oelschlagel. In 1908, a resident ice-ballet company was created by Leo Bartuschek at the Berlin Eis Palast. Hans Witté, who was later to become London's leading ice-show refrigerating engineer, was one of the Berlin performers. He says skating ballets were presented regularly for four years and that, good though they were, the company hedged its bets at first by planting professional applauders among the audience.

As a result, the first sizeable theatrical skating productions, as distinct from a series of exhibition performers, was presented at the Admiral Palast, Berlin, in the summer of 1913. It was a style of musical comedy, titled *Flirting at St Moritz*. Stanley Fryett, who became something of a skating historian, was a young instructor at the Admiral Palast at the time. Many years later, when manager of the Dundee ice rink in Scotland, he assured me that the show was worthy of its historic importance, with more than a hundred performers in the original cast. The star was Charlotte, a seventeen-year-old from Berlin.

In the United States, the idea of small ice rinks for skating cabarets in the dining-rooms of leading hotels was introduced by Frank Bearing in 1914, with notable success at the Sherman Hotel in Chicago. Other hotels quickly followed suit and, in 1915, the obvious popularity of this new vogue encouraged the American impresario, Charles Dillingham, to import the German production from the Admiral Palast and re-stage it at the New York Hippodrome, then the largest playhouse in America. On a frozen stage measuring ninety by forty-five feet, *Flirting at St Moritz* was booked for six weeks — and ran for three years, playing to twice daily audiences of six thousand.

Charlotte, whose surname was quickly dropped and whose 'Dying Swan' was coached by Anna Pavlova, became the toast of New York. She inspired the opening of many new rinks and a profusion of hotel ice cabarets, including one at the Waldorf-Astoria in New York. Charlotte was now almost a legend. She became the first skating film star in a six-episode serial called *The Frozen Warning*, a title inspired by an incident in the story

Sonja Henie at the zenith of her screen fame, as seen in the 20th Century-Fox film, 'Iceland', made in 1942. Her looks and attractive skating in simple, romantic stories were enhanced by her English dialogue in a Norwegian accent which her fans loved. Her glamorous skating dresses, glittering tiaras and flamboyantly plumed headwear set fashion trends for many ice revues to follow.

when a sinister message, 'Spies', was traced by her skates on the ice.

Maribel Vinson, the United States Olympic skater and coach, who subsequently performed with Charlotte in Switzerland and became skating correspondent for the *New York Times*, wrote in 1951: 'Charlotte was the first woman to do an axel jump and there are many who swear that she was the greatest woman skater who has ever lived, years ahead of her time, limited not by ability but by invention, from doing all the double jumps of today.' Charlotte was a masterly exponent of the camel spin and is credited, too, with inventing the death spiral in pair skating.

It was not until 1926 that skating was first presented in an English theatre — a production called *Ballets on Ice*, on the stage of the London Coliseum. This was followed by an ice presentation in 1930 at the London Stoll in Holborn, where now stands the Royalty Theatre. The first skating musical in Britain, *Arabian Nights* in 1932 at the Westover Ice Rink, Bournemouth, instigated yearly summer shows at that venue. The year 1936 proved a memorable milestone in the annals of theatrical skating. In Britain, Claude Langdon presented his first ice show, *Marina*, at Brighton Sports Stadium. In America, the regular touring ice revue was born when, on 7 November at Tulsa, Oklahoma, *Ice Follies* opened under the auspices of Oscar Johnson, a chemist, Eddie Shipstad, a typewriter salesman, and brother Roy Shipstad, a garage attendant. They never needed to return to their former trades because *Ice Follies* is still running.

But in May, 1936, Sonja Henie turned professional and did more to promote the popularity and public awareness of skating than any one person ever had, with her starring rôle in the first full-length skating feature film — a simple, romantic story called *One in a Million*. It won so very many hearts and brought skating, as no other medium then could, into the minds of multitudes. Younger readers would hardly regret taking the opportunity to see any repeat showing of this Twentieth Century Fox film. The same goes for any of the skating films Sonja starred in afterwards, namely, *Thin Ice, Happy Landings, My Lucky Star, Second Fiddle, Everything Happens at Night, Sun Valley Serenade* (with Glenn Miller), *Iceland, Wintertime, It's a Pleasure, Countess of Monte Cristo* and *Hello, London.*

Sonja, even when an amateur, set the lead to inspire a practical shortening of the skating skirt. The fashions she set in her films were similarly influential. From her father she inherited a keen business sense. She grew to be universally loved on the ice, and respected off it. She never lost the taste for battle and toured the world with her own lavish, lucrative ice revues, heavily insuring her legs and amassing a considerable fortune because of her commercial acumen as well as her great artistry. Her grace and femininity nobody could deny, but she was also free from affectation and a hard bargainer. Ironically, her wealth was of no avail when, in 1969, leukaemia sadly terminated skating's most famous personality at the age of fifty-seven.

In 1937, London's most ambitious ice ballet was appropriately performed on a specially built temporary rink at the Royal Opera House, Covent Garden. The hundred-strong cast included Belita, turning professional for this when only fourteen. The following year, the London Coliseum presented *St Moritz*, a spectacle which excited impresarios by clearly revealing the potentialities of ice in the theatre. Claude Langdon, preferring to stay with rinks, re-staged his earlier Brighton success, *Marina*, at Blackpool Ice Drome in 1937 and at London's Empress Hall, Earls Court, in 1938. Alas, British progress, thus stimulated, was destined to be put on ice in a sadly different sense, because of the advent of World War II, although Hitler failed to curb ice shows in the United States.

Ice Capades, the second major touring skating revue company to be formed, with John H. Harris as senior executive, was launched on 16 June, 1940, at the New Orleans Municipal Auditorium. The third great combine, *Holiday on Ice*, instigated by Emery Gilbert, Morris Chalfen and George Tyson, began in 1945 as part of the Wisconsin State Fair at Milwaukee.

Belita, the British skating film star who followed in Sonja Henie's wake, is seen here in the Pathé picture, 'Suspense'. After competing in the 1936 Olympics at Garmisch-Partenkirchen, Germany, Belita turned professional when only 14 to appear the following year in London's first major ice ballet. This was held on a specially constructed tank at the Royal Opera House, Covent Garden.

The three giants, *Ice Follies*, *Ice Capades* and *Holiday on Ice*, naturally became zealous rivals but, significantly, there has always been plenty of business for all of them. At first, their performances were confined to existing rinks, but by the early 1950s each had acquired equipment to instal full-sized portable rinks, colloquially termed tanks, in arenas without a permanent ice surface — thus expanding their choice of venue to every large stadium. From the outset right up to the present day, they have keenly competed for the best available skating talent and, at every major amateur championship, their executives and scouts are poised, like vultures waiting for their prey, with contract forms at the ready.

Blackpool Ice Drome, which was built and designed primarily for ice shows in 1937, was the only place in Britain to stage any ice entertainments during World War II. The first of Leonard Thompson's resident *Ice Parade* revues was presented there in 1940, and new editions have been held there every summer since. But the end of hostilities cleared the decks for a revolution in British show skating. The great revival was sparked off by theatre magnate Tom Arnold's *Hot Ice*, produced by Armand Perren at Brighton in 1945. It was followed a year later by *Ice Caprice*, a springboard to the bigger events which just had to come. In 1946, Arnold transformed the London Stoll into a regular ice theatre, in the same way as New York's Center Theatre had been converted in 1940. Arnold's producer, Gerald Palmer, was to become Europe's leading ice-show impresario — with one-hundred-and-thirty productions to his credit.

Cecilia Colledge starred in that first Stoll venture, masterminding an ice ballet, *Midsummer Night's Dream*. That beautiful, deceptive ease and technically perfect precision which personified her every movement on those silver blades marked Cecilia as a proficient product of hard practice,

This colourful scene from a 'Holiday on Ice' extravaganza illustrates how a cold ice rink can be transformed in the mind to a warm Latin American setting.

Cecilia Colledge starring with Bob Caroll in a delectable ballet sequence to Mendelssohn's 'Midsummer Night' in 'Ice Revue', which opened in 1946 at the Stoll Theatre in Kingsway, London. Cecilia was a proficient product of unstintingly hard practice and her efforts in this show helped spark Britain's post-war theatrical skating boom.

performing exquisitely to the letter of the text book. *Stars on Ice* followed at the Stoll in 1948, co-starring Daphne Walker and two American acts, the sensationally acrobatic Adele Inge and The Three Rookies, the best true skating comics I have ever seen. In 1949, Cecilia returned to *Ice Vogues* and was joined by comedian Richard Hearne, famed on the conventional stage for his elderly gentleman creation, Mr Pastry. On dress rehearsal night, Dicky invited me to watch him prepare the celebrated Mr Pastry make-up, for which, as millions of televiewers have seen since for themselves, no wig was ever used, his own hair being carefully whitened for every performance.

'Has Cecilia been teaching you?' I asked him that night, knowing that the show required him to skate round with her in the guise of a shaky beginner in true Pastry tradition.

'No,' he replied. 'I've never skated before and I've made a special point of *not* having any lessons or even trying it out at rehearsals, because my falling about will look much more realistic that way.' This was the philosophy of a great trouper who, like so many successful comedians, took his work very seriously — despite the price, in this instance, of many tender contusions in embarrassing places.

Ice Vogues ended the great Stoll run of successes, but not because there was any loss of interest. On the contrary, the success and nature of theatrical skating was such that a conventional theatre's restricted size of auditorium and stage could no longer compete in London with the elaborate spectacles about to be presented at the large arenas of Earls Court, Wembley and Harringay. It became evident that the discerning London show-going public would not be content only with revues indefinitely. However good the acts, there was a limit to the variety and element of surprise. A story was the obvious answer, and it was an easy, natural move to put pantomime on skates.

The link of pantomime with a wintry ice atmosphere was ideally suitable for the Christmas season. That this triumphant development should be confined to Britain, however, is simply explained by a fact which many Britons do not appreciate — that Christmas pantomime is a tradition peculiar to their country and virtually unknown elsewhere. Although the first sizeable ice pantomime on record had been enacted at the old Purley rink in 1933, the first performances of this kind to be staged in the 'grand manner' was Claude Langdon's *Cinderella* at the Empress Hall, Earls Court, and Tom Arnold's *Aladdin* at Brighton Sports Stadium, both in 1949. And, in the summer of 1950, history was made at Harringay Arena, in north London, where the first full-length musical ever to be presented on ice — the first ice operetta, in fact, *Rose Marie* — had in the title part the petite, light-footed Canadian, Barbara Ann Scott, partnered by Michael Kirby. I shall always remember the effective moonlight march of the scarlet-coated Mounties.

The tremendous success in 1950 of Wembley's first ice pantomime, *Dick Whittington*, may be measured by the fact that six hundred thousand patrons saw it in a three-month season. Opened appropriately by the Lord Mayor of London, it displayed a magnificent array of rich fifteenth-century splendour, which captured the majestic atmosphere and pageantry of city tradition. Presented by Sir Arthur Elvin with Gerald Palmer producing, it heralded an era of lavish, expensive spectacles at Wembley, whose resplendent wealth of costumes and décor surely set a new precedent in any form of show business, and which a conventional theatre's economy could never conceivably match. By curious coincidence, the part of the Fairy Princess was played by Elizabeth Whittington, a direct descendant of the real Dick Whittington, thrice Lord Mayor of London.

Concurrently at the Empress Hall that winter was another great Langdon presentation, *Babes in the Wood*, led by film star Belita as Robin Hood. Belita Jepson-Turner was born at the little English village of Nether Wallop, in Hampshire, deriving her unusual name from her great-grandfather's Argentine ranch called 'La Belita'. Skating her way to the top of the film firmament had not been easy for her, following so soon in the wake of the great Sonja, but Belita made many films with a skating theme, including *Silver Skates*, *Lady Let's Dance*, *Suspense*, *The Gangster* and *The Hunted*, at the same time achieving fame as a ballet dancer, the knowledge acquired from this appreciably assisting her recognized ability as a show skater of the first order.

The appeal of ice shows in Britain reached a remarkable peak during the 1950s. Each Wembley presentation strived to emulate and improve upon its predecessor. Moving décor became progressively more ambitious. One recalls scale-model galleons in full sail under fire, a half-scale model of the Comet airliner emitting flames from its four jet engines, a model battleship with a quarterdeck nearly half the size of a real light cruiser, and a rocket-propelled flying saucer sixty feet in circumference. There was once a waterfall thirty feet high, and several times the more commonly seen dancing waters — cascading fountains, shooting water in hundreds of multi-coloured jets which altered shape and danced to music. Eight illuminated Pullman dining-cars once drew into a realistic railway station. The Royal Tournament's intricate equestrianism was portrayed by eighty-four skaters skilfully arrayed as illusory horses and riders. Fluorescent ballets under ultra-violet lighting effects became commonplace.

Perhaps Wembley's best-ever ice show was *Chu Chin Chow* in 1953. Not a display of advanced skating technique, it was Oscar Asche's record-breaking stage musical transposed, as faithfully as seemed practicable, on to the frozen surface, with the emphisis on oriental spectacle and all the consequent luxury that is afforded by, and indeed necessary to attract, some eight thousand well satisfied customers at each performance. The lavish costume designs were almost beyond criticism and did much to capture Baghdad's colourful legendary atmosphere, together with sumptuous, yet tasteful scenery that included a proscenium eighty-five feet high and nearly three hundred feet wide.

Oozing with calculable personality and forever radiating obvious enthusiasm, the lithe and slender Gloria Nord skated the rôle of the pixie-like Marjanah. She proved that, from the waist upwards, the scantily attired blonde queen of Wembley's inventory had no peers in this particular field and indefatigably employed arms and hands throughout with consummate skill. This, possibly, was theatrical skating's finest hour. A sequel to this

Barbara Ann Scott, the winsomely diminutive Canadian star of 'Rose Marie' in 1950 at Harringay Arena, north London, was so successful in this, her professional debut, that the show ran for a second year.

spectacle was the selection of Gloria to perform before the Queen on skates for the first time in a Royal Variety Show, at the London Coliseum on 2 November 1953. What began with the official choice of one artist culminated with a supporting ice corps de ballet to dress the stage for Gloria's specially prepared solo to Charles Chaplin's music from the film, *Limelight.*

Big names from other realms of show business, notably comedians, quickly jumped on the bandwagon of a medium that was now able to match offers from the stage. Norman Wisdom, Ted Ray, Frankie Vaughan, Max Wall, Bob and Alf Pearson, Tommy Trinder, Jimmy Jewel and Ben Warriss are but a few who spring to mind. Sometimes the 'imports' were excessive, and I recall gently criticizing unsuitable acts with such comments as 'the dexterous conjuring is worth bringing binoculars to discern', and 'you need a flair for flame-throwing, but not ice'.

Sometimes three or four ice shows played in Greater London simultaneously, with perhaps another half-dozen in the provinces. The skate-mindedness of theatregoers was then such that I often wonder if there was a true-life foundation for the story of the woman who stopped outside the Earls Court Motor Show and asked: 'Is it on ice?' Sometimes, I, too, had the amusing pleasure of being the first to tell American skaters that, in British pantomime, the leading male rôle is (or was then) played by a girl and that of the Dame by a man. In Britain, much more than anywhere else, far more was now required of show skaters than the mere ability to skate pleasingly. In pantomimes and musicals, they were schooled into becoming dramatic actors and actresses. In the smaller theatres, the skaters were sometimes specially trained to speak their own dialogue, but in the most spacious arena productions each leading character usually comprised two different people — the miming skater synchronizing every movement with a 'disembodied' voice, the story being embellished by the accompaniment of large orchestras and choirs.

It was quite surprising to learn that many who visited these large-scale pantomimes or musicals on ice went away still quite convinced that the skaters *sung* beautifully. I suppose to some non-skaters the thought just did not occur that in these vast stadia no voice could carry audibly to all parts without personal microphones (though some were used occasionally with limited success), quite apart from the fact that no skater could sing while performing the more energetic turns, lifts and gyrations. There was, of course, no intention whatsoever of deceiving the audience, as the printed programmes plainly confirmed. Patrons were merely asked to pretend to themselves that the skater was speaking, in order to lend reality to the story. During rehearsals, skaters and voice, commonly termed the dubber, learned by painstaking practice to synchronize their sound and vision. So the skaters were dumb — on the ice, that is. I have a private theory about their making up for lost time off it!

The summer of 1954 was another milestone in the further development of full-length musicals on ice, when Ivor Novello's *The Dancing Years* was staged at Wembley. I had thought of Ivor frequently as a lone, wistful figure with just a piano on an unadorned wartime ENSA platform in Belgium, when he introduced and sang 'a new tune that I hope may one day be the theme of a new musical play'. For the first time, to an enraptured audience of air-force blue we heard, sung by its composer. 'We'll Gather Lilacs', the melody that was afterwards to become the hit of *Perchance to Dream*.

Before the critical Wembley concourse, *The Dancing Years* was a remarkably faithful transposition on to skates of Ivor's best-loved musical, with 'We'll Gather Lilacs' added. Not to be outdone, the Empress Hall at the same time staged *White Horse Inn*, with an almost authentic replica of the hostel and village of St Wolfgang in the Austrian Tyrol. Another memorable success was Walt Disney's *Snow White and the Seven Dwarfs* on Wembley ice, its unfolding story was so absorbing that Snow White was consistently implored by the audience not to eat the poisoned apple.

While Britain almost exclusively exploited the full-length story in ice shows with a continuity theme throughout the entire performance, America always led the way with a streamlined manner of slick timing in skating revues, particularly in presentation of ensembles. It is this format which has stood the test of time. Since the early 1950s, when quicker ways were found to instal better portable rinks safely in arenas lacking ice — it can now be done in less than ten hours — the big three North American companies have continued to thrive. While *Ice Follies* and *Ice Capades* have ventured abroad only occasionally, *Holiday on Ice* has broadened its horizons to become a colossus of show business. As the Guinness Book of Records enumerates, *Holiday on Ice* now stages the world's most costly live entertainment with up to seven productions playing simultaneously around the globe, drawing twenty million spectators paying over forty million dollars in a year. The total skating and other staff exceeds nine hundred.

Another modern variation of theatrical skating is the one-off TV ice spectacular — money-spinning presentations which, in the United States, have starred such performers as Peggy Fleming, Karen Magnussen, Toller Cranston and John Curry with very favourable impact.

This scene from a 'Holiday on Ice' production number illustrates the detail of costumery and outsize decor adapted to suit a large arena. In this case a delightful excerpt from 'Alice in Wonderland' designed to appeal to family audiences.

Medallists

Olympic Figure Skating Competitions

Men

	Gold	Silver	Bronze
1908￼London	Ulrich Salchow￼(Sweden)	Richard Johansson￼(Sweden)	Per Thorén￼(Sweden)
1920￼Antwerp	Gillis Grafström￼(Sweden)	Andreas Krogh￼(Norway)	Martin Stixrud￼(Norway)
1924￼Chamonix	Gillis Grafström￼(Sweden)	Willy Böckl￼(Austria)	Georg Gautschi￼(Switzerland)
1928￼St Moritz	Gillis Grafström￼(Sweden)	Willy Böckl￼(Austria)	Bobby van Zeebroeck￼(Belgium)
1932￼Lake Placid	Karl Schäfer￼(Austria)	Gillis Grafström￼(Sweden)	Montgomery Wilson￼(Canada)
1936￼Garmisch	Karl Schäfer￼(Austria)	Ernst Baier￼(Germany)	Felix Kasper￼(Austria)
1948￼St Moritz	Dick Button￼(USA)	Hans Gerschwiler￼(Switzerland)	Edi Rada￼(Austria)
1952￼Oslo	Dick Button￼(USA)	Helmut Seibt￼(Austria)	James Grogan￼(USA)
1956￼Cortina	Hayes Jenkins￼(USA)	Ronald Robertson￼(USA)	David Jenkins￼(USA)
1960￼Squaw Valley	David Jenkins￼(USA)	Carol Divin￼(Czechoslovakia)	Donald Jackson￼(Canada)
1964￼Innsbruck	Manfred Schnelldorfer￼(Germany)	Alain Calmat￼(France)	Scott Allen￼(USA)
1968￼Grenoble	Wolfgang Schwarz￼(Austria)	Tim Wood￼(USA)	Patrick Pera￼(France)
1972￼Sapporo	Ondrej Nepela￼(Czechoslovakia)	Sergei Chetverukhin￼(USSR)	Patrick Pera￼(France)
1976￼Innsbruck	John Curry￼(Great Britain)	Vladimir Kovalev￼(USSR)	Toller Cranston￼(Canada)
1980￼Lake Placid	Robin Cousins￼(Great Britain)	Jan Hoffman￼(East Germany)	Charles Tickner￼(USA)

Women

	Gold	Silver	Bronze
1908￼London	Madge Syers￼(Great Britain)	Elsa Rendschmidt￼(Germany)	Dorothy Grennhough-Smith￼(Great Britain)
1920￼Antwerp	Magda Julin-Mauroy￼(Sweden)	Svea Norén￼(Sweden)	Theresa Weld￼(USA)
1924￼Chamonix	Herma Plank-Szabo￼(Austria)	Beatrix Loughran￼(USA)	Ethel Muckelt￼(Great Britain)
1928￼St Moritz	Sonja Henie￼(Norway)	Fritzi Burger￼(Austria)	Beatrix Loughran￼(USA)
1932￼Lake Placid	Sonja Henie￼(Norway)	Fritzi Burger￼(Austria)	Maribel Vinson￼(USA)
1936￼Garmisch	Sonja Henie￼(Norway)	Cecilia Colledge￼(Great Britain)	Vivi-Anne Hultén￼(Sweden)
1948￼St Moritz	Barbara Ann Scott￼(Canada)	Eva Pawlik￼(Austria)	Jeannette Altwegg￼(Great Britain)
1952￼Oslo	Jeannette Altwegg￼(Great Britain)	Tenley Albright￼(USA)	Jacqueline du Bief￼(France)

Graham Sharp, Britain's world champion in 1939. His then highly promising career was abruptly curtailed by a war which killed his runner-up and compatriot, Freddie Tomlins. Eight times national title winner, Graham was his country's only men's world champion until John Curry's success 37 years later.

	Gold	Silver	Bronze
1956 Cortina	Tenley Albright (USA)	Carol Heiss (USA)	Ingrid Wendl (Austria)
1960 Squaw Valley	Carol Heiss (USA)	Sjoukje Dijkstra (Netherlands)	Barbara Roles (USA)
1964 Innsbruck	Sjoukje Dijkstra (Netherlands)	Regine Heitzer (Austria)	Petra Burka (Canada)
1968 Grenoble	Peggy Fleming (USA)	Gabriele Seyfert (East Germany)	Hana Maskova (Czechoslovakia)
1972 Sapporo	Beatrix Schuba (Austria)	Karen Magnussen (Canada)	Janet Lynn (USA)
1976 Innsbruck	Dorothy Hamill (USA)	Dianne de Leeuw (Netherlands)	Christine Errath (East Germany)
1980 Lake Placid	Anett Pötzsch (East Germany)	Linda Fratianne (USA)	Dagmar Lurz (West Germany)

Hayes Jenkins, pictured during an exhibition in Prague, was four times world champion for the United States and won the Olympic gold medal in 1956. His younger brother David succeeded him with one Olympic and three world titles and Hayes's future wife, Carol Heiss, won an Olympic and five world titles — quite a family haul.

Pairs

	Gold	Silver	Bronze
1908 London	Heinrich Burger Anna Hübler (Germany)	James Johnson Phyllis Johnson (Great Britain)	Edgar Syers Madge Syers (Great Britain)
1920 Antwerp	Walter Jakobsson Ludowika Eilers (Finland)	Yngvar Bryn Alexia Schöyen (Norway)	Basil Williams Phyllis Johnson (Great Britain)
1924 Chamonix	Alfred Berger Helene Engelmann (Austria)	Walter Jakobsson Ludowika Eilers (Finland)	Pierre Brunet Andrée Joly (France)
1928 St Moritz	Pierre Brunet Andrée Joly (France)	Otto Kaiser Lilly Scholz (Austria)	Ludwig Wrede Melitta Brunner (Austria)
1932 Lake Placid	Pierre Brunet Andrée Joly (France)	Sherwin Badger Beatrix Loughran (USA)	Lászlo Szollás Emilie Rotter (Hungary)
1936 Garmisch	Ernst Baier Maxie Herber (Germany)	Erich Pausin Ilse Pausin (Austria)	Lászlo Szollás Emilie Rotter (Hungary)
1948 St Moritz	Pierre Baugniet Micheline Lannoy (Belgium)	Ede Király Andrea Kékesy (Hungary)	Wallace Distelmeyer Suzanne Morrow (Canada)
1952 Oslo	Paul Falk Ria Baran (Germany)	Peter Kennedy Karol Kennedy (USA)	Laszlo Nagy Marianne Nagy (Hungary)
1956 Cortina	Kurt Oppelt Sissy Schwarz (Austria)	Norris Bowden Frances Dafoe (Canada)	Laszlo Nagy Marianne Nagy (Hungary)
1960 Squaw Valley	Robert Paul Barbara Wagner (Canada)	Hans-Jürgen Bäumler Marika Kilius (Germany)	Ronald Ludington Nancy Ludington (USA)
1964 Innsbruck	Oleg Protopopov Ludmila Belousova (USSR)	Hans-Jürgen Bäumler Marika Kilius (Germany)	Guy Revell Debbi Wilkes (Canada)
1968 Grenoble	Oleg Protopopov Ludmila Belousova (USSR)	Aleksandr Gorelik Tatjana Zhuk (USSR)	Wolfgang Danne Margot Glockshuber (West Germany)
1972 Sapporo	Alexsei Ulanov Irina Rodnina (USSR)	Andrei Suraikin Ludmila Smirnova (USSR)	Uwe Kagelmann Manuela Gross (East Germany)
1976 Innsbruck	Aleksandr Zaitsev Irina Rodnina (USSR)	Rolf Oesterreich Romy Kermer (East Germany)	Uwe Kagelmann Manuela Gross (East Germany)
1980 Lake Placid	Aleksandr Zaitsev Irina Rodnina (USSR)	Sergei Shakrai Marina Cherkasova (USSR)	Uwe Bewersdorff Manuela Mager (East Germany)

Ice Dance

	Gold	Silver	Bronze
1976 Innsbruck	Aleksandr Gorshkov Ludmila Pakhomova (USSR)	Andrei Minenkov Irina Moiseeva (USSR)	Jim Millns Colleen O'Connor (USA)
1980 Lake Placid	Gennadi Karponosov Natalia Linichuk (USSR)	Andras Sallay Krisztina Regoczy (Hungary)	Andrei Minenkov Irina Moiseeva (USSR)

World Figure Skating Championships

Men

	Gold	Silver	Bronze
1896 Leningrad	Gilbert Fuchs (Germany)	Gustav Hügel (Austria)	Georg Sanders (Russia)
1897 Stockholm	Gustav Hügel (Austria)	Ulrich Salchow (Sweden)	Johan Lefstad (Norway)
1898 London	Henning Grenander (Sweden)	Gustav Hügel (Austria)	Gilbert Fuchs (Germany)
1899 Davos	Gustav Hügel (Austria)	Ulrich Salchow (Sweden)	Edgar Syers (Great Britain)
1900 Davos	Gustav Hügel (Austria)	Ulrich Salchow (Sweden)	—
1901 Stockholm	Ulrich Salchow (Sweden)	Gilbert Fuchs (Germany)	—
1902 London	Ulrich Salchow (Sweden)	Madge Syers (Great Britain)	Martin Gordan (Germany)
1903 Leningrad	Ulrich Salchow (Sweden)	Nicolai Panin (Russia)	Max Bohatsch (Austria)
1904 Berlin	Ulrich Salchow (Sweden)	Heinrich Burger (Germany)	Martin Gordan (Germany)
1905 Stockholm	Ulrich Salchow (Sweden)	Max Bohatsch (Austria)	Per Thorén (Sweden)
1906 Munich	Gilbert Fuchs (Germany)	Heinrich Burger (Germany)	Bror Meyer (Sweden)
1907 Vienna	Ulrich Salchow (Sweden)	Max Bohatsch (Austria)	Gilbert Fuchs (Germany)
1908 Troppau	Ulrich Salchow (Sweden)	Gilbert Fuchs (Germany)	Heinrich Burger (Germany)
1909 Stockholm	Ulrich Salchow (Sweden)	Per Thorén (Sweden)	Ernest Herz (Austria)
1910 Davos	Ulrich Salchow (Sweden)	Werner Rittberger (Germany)	Andor Szende (Hungary)
1911 Berlin	Ulrich Salchow (Sweden)	Werner Rittberger (Germany)	Fritz Kachler (Austria)
1912 Manchester	Fritz Kachler (Austria)	Werner Rittberger (Germany)	Andor Szende (Hungary)
1913 Vienna	Fritz Kachler (Austria)	Willy Böckl (Austria)	Andor Szende (Hungary)
1914 Helsinki	Gösta Sandahl (Sweden)	Fritz Kachler (Austria)	Willy Böckl (Austria)
1922 Stockholm	Gillis Grafström (Sweden)	Fritz Kachler (Austria)	Willy Böckl (Austria)
1923 Vienna	Fritz Kachler (Austria)	Willy Böckl (Austria)	Gösta Sandahl (Sweden)
1924 Manchester	Gillis Grafström (Sweden)	Willy Böckl (Austria)	Ernst Oppacher (Austria)
1925 Vienna	Willy Böckl (Austria)	Fritz Kachler (Austria)	Otto Preissecker (Austria)

1926 Berlin	Willy Böckl (Austria)	Otto Preissecker (Austria)	John Page (Great Britain)
1927 Davos	Willy Böckl (Austria)	Otto Preissecker (Austria)	Karl Schäfer (Austria)
1928 Berlin	Willy Böckl (Austria)	Karl Schäfer (Austria)	Hugo Distler (Austria)
1929 London	Gillis Grafström (Sweden)	Karl Schäfer (Austria)	Ludwig Wrede (Austria)
1930 New York	Karl Schäfer (Austria)	Roger Turner (USA)	Georg Gautschi (Switzerland)
1931 Berlin	Karl Schäfer (Austria)	Roger Turner (USA)	Ernst Baier (Germany)
1932 Montreal	Karl Schäfer (Austria)	Montgomery Wilson (Canada)	Ernst Baier (Germany)
1933 Zurich	Karl Schäfer (Austria)	Ernst Baier (Germany)	Markus Nikkanen (Finland)
1934 Stockholm	Karl Schäfer (Austria)	Ernst Baier (Germany)	Erich Erdös (Austria)
1935 Budapest	Karl Schäfer (Austria)	Jack Dunn (Great Britain)	Dénes Pataky (Hungary)
1936 Paris	Karl Schäfer (Austria)	Graham Sharp (Great Britain)	Felix Kaspar (Austria)
1937 Vienna	Felix Kaspar (Austria)	Graham Sharp (Great Britain)	Elemér Tertak (Hungary)
1938 Berlin	Felix Kaspar (Austria)	Graham Sharp (Great Britain)	Herbert Alward (Austria)
1939 Budapest	Graham Sharp (Great Britain)	Freddie Tomlins (Great Britain)	Horst Faber (Germany)
1947 Stockholm	Hans Gerschwiler (Switzerland)	Dick Button (USA)	Arthur Apfel (Great Britain)
1948 Davos	Dick Button (USA)	Hans Gerschwiler (Switzerland)	Ede Király (Hungary)
1949 Paris	Dick Button (USA)	Ede Király (Hungary)	Edi Rada (Austria)
1950 London	Dick Button (USA)	Ede Király (Hungary)	Hayes Jenkins (USA)

John Curry, for once skating outdoors, looks as always the stylist. Whether in figures or free skating, John gained the greatest satisfaction from correct detail, as he saw it, of every head, body, arm, leg, hand and finger movement. Even the facial expression was used constantly to interpret the mood to suit his music.

Don McPherson of Canada makes an ecstatic split jump high above the Davos rink in the Swiss Alps. Don was world champion in 1963.

1951 Milan	Dick Button (USA)	James Grogan (USA)	Helmut Seibt (Austria)
1952 Paris	Dick Button (USA)	James Grogan (USA)	Hayes Jenkins (USA)
1953 Davos	Hayes Jenkins (USA)	James Grogan (USA)	Carlo Fassi (Italy)
1954 Oslo	Hayes Jenkins (USA)	James Grogan (USA)	Alain Giletti (France)
1955 Vienna	Hayes Jenkins (USA)	Ronald Robertson (USA)	David Jenkins (USA)
1956 Garmisch	Hayes Jenkins (USA)	Ronald Robertson (USA)	David Jenkins (USA)
1957 Colorado Springs	David Jenkins (USA)	Tim Brown (USA)	Charles Snelling (Canada)
1958 Paris	David Jenkins (USA)	Tim Brown (USA)	Alain Giletti (France)
1959 Colorado Springs	David Jenkins (USA)	Donald Jackson (Canada)	Tim Brown (USA)
1960 Vancouver	Alain Giletti (France)	Donald Jackson (Canada)	Alain Calmat (France)
1962 Prague	Donald Jackson (Canada)	Carol Divin (Czechoslovakia)	Alain Calmat (France)
1963 Cortina	Donald McPherson (Canada)	Alain Calmat (France)	Manfred Schnelldorfer (West Germany)
1964 Dortmund	Manfred Schnelldorfer (West Germany)	Alain Calmat (France)	Carol Divin (Czechoslovakia)
1965 Colorado Springs	Alain Calmat (France)	Scott Allen (USA)	Donald Knight (Canada)
1966 Davos	Emmerich Danzer (Austria)	Wolfgang Schwarz (Austria)	Gary Visconti (USA)
1967 Vienna	Emmerich Danzer (Austria)	Wolfgang Schwarz (Austria)	Gary Visconti (USA)
1968 Geneva	Emmerich Danzer (Austria)	Tim Wood (USA)	Patrick Pera (France)
1969 Colorado Springs	Tim Wood (USA)	Ondrej Nepela (Czechoslovakia)	Patrick Pera (France)
1970 Ljubljana	Tim Wood (USA)	Ondrej Nepela (Czechoslovakia)	Gunter Zöller (East Germany)
1971 Lyon	Ondrej Nepela (Czechoslovakia)	Patrick Pera (France)	Sergei Chetverukhin (USSR)
1972 Calgary	Ondrej Nepela (Czechoslovakia)	Sergei Chetverukhin (USSR)	Vladimir Kovalev (USSR)
1973 Bratislava	Ondrej Nepela (Czechoslovakia)	Sergei Chetverukhin (USSR)	Jan Hoffmann (East Germany)
1974 Munich	Jan Hoffmann (East Germany)	Sergei Volkov (USSR)	Toller Cranston (Canada)
1975 Colorado Springs	Sergei Volkov (USSR)	Vladimir Kovalev (USSR)	John Curry (Great Britain)
1976 Gothenburg	John Curry (Great Britain)	Vladimir Kovalev (USSR)	Jan Hoffmann (East Germany)
1977 Tokyo	Vladimir Kovalev (USSR)	Jan Hoffmann (East Germany)	Minoru Sano (Japan)
1978 Ottawa	Charles Tickner (USA)	Jan Hoffmann (East Germany)	Robin Cousins (Great Britain)
1979 Vienna	Vladimir Kovalev (USSR)	Robin Cousins (Great Britain)	Jan Hoffmann (East Germany)
1980 Dortmund	Jan Hoffman (East Germany)	Robin Cousins (Great Britain)	Charles Tickner (USA)

Women

	Gold	Silver	Bronze
1906 Davos	Madge Syers (Great Britain)	Jenny Herz (Austria)	Lily Kronberger (Hungary)
1907 Vienna	Madge Syers (Great Britain)	Jenny Herz (Austria)	Lily Kronberger (Hungary)
1908 Troppau	Lily Kronberger (Hungary)	Elsa Rendschmidt (Germany)	—
1909 Budapest	Lily Kronberger (Hungary)	—	—
1910 Berlin	Lily Kronberger (Hungary)	Elsa Rendschmidt (Germany)	—
1911 Vienna	Lily Kronberger (Hungary)	Opika von Horvath (Hungary)	Ludowika Eilers (Germany)
1912 Davos	Opika von Horvath (Hungary)	Dorothy Grennhough-Smith (Great Britain)	Phyllis Johnson (Great Britain)
1913 Stockholm	Opika von Horvath (Hungary)	Phyllis Johnson (Great Britain)	Svea Norén (Sweden)
1914 St Moritz	Opika von Horvath (Hungary)	Angela Hanka (Austria)	Phyllis Johnson (Great Britain)
1922 Stockholm	Herma Plank-Szabo (Austria)	Svea Norén (Sweden)	Margot Moe (Norway)
1923 Vienna	Herma Plank-Szabo (Austria)	Gisela Reichmann (Austria)	Svea Norén (Sweden)
1924 Oslo	Herma Plank-Szabo (Austria)	Ellen Brockhöfft (Germany)	Beatrix Loughran (USA)
1925 Davos	Herma Jaross-Szabo (Austria)	Ellen Brockhöfft (Germany)	Elisabeth Böckel (Germany)
1926 Stockholm	Herma Jaross-Szabo (Austria)	Sonja Henie (Norway)	Kathleen Shaw (Great Britain)
1927 Oslo	Sonja Henie (Norway)	Herma Jaross-Szabo (Austria)	Karen Simensen (Norway)
1928 London	Sonja Henie (Norway)	Maribel Vinson (USA)	Fritzi Burger (Austria)
1929 Budapest	Sonja Henie (Norway)	Fritzi Burger (Austria)	Melitta Brunner (Austria)
1930 New York	Sonja Henie (Norway)	Cecil Smith (Canada)	Maribel Vinson (USA)
1931 Berlin	Sonja Henie (Norway)	Hilde Holovsky (Austria)	Fritzi Burger (Austria)
1932 Montreal	Sonja Henie (Norway)	Fritzi Burger (Austria)	Constance Samuel (Canada)
1933 Stockholm	Sonja Henie (Norway)	Vivi-Anne Hultén (Sweden)	Hilde Holovsky (Austria)
1934 Oslo	Sonja Henie (Norway)	Megan Taylor (Great Britain)	Liselotte Landbeck (Austria)
1935 Vienna	Sonja Henie (Norway)	Cecilia Colledge (Great Britain)	Vivi-Anne Hultén (Sweden)
1936 Paris	Sonja Henie (Norway)	Megan Taylor (Great Britain)	Vivi-Anne Hultén (Sweden)
1937 London	Cecilia Colledge (Great Britain)	Megan Taylor (Great Britain)	Vivi-Anne Hultén (Sweden)
1938 Stockholm	Megan Taylor (Great Britain)	Cecilia Colledge (Great Britain)	Hedy Stenuf (USA)
1939 Prague	Megan Taylor (Great Britain)	Hedy Stenuf (USA)	Daphne Walker (Great Britain)
1947 Stockholm	Barbara Ann Scott (Canada)	Daphne Walker (Great Britain)	Gretchen Merrill (USA)

A young Megan Taylor, later to become Britain's world champion in 1938 and 1939, gets to grips with a 'polar bear' in a novel exhibition at Lake Placid, New York. Megan's father, Phil, coached his daughter and Graham Sharp to world titles — and then achieved fame as a show skater on stilts.

Karen Magnussen winning the world title for Canada at Bratislava in 1973, after gaining Olympic silver at Sapporo the year before. Karen later appeared in lucrative spectaculars on North American television.

1948 Davos	Barbara Ann Scott (Canada)	Eva Pawlik (Austria)	Jirina Nekolova (Czechoslovakia)
1949 Paris	Aja Vrzanova (Czechoslovakia)	Yvonne Sherman (USA)	Jeannette Altwegg (Great Britain)
1950 London	Aja Vrzanova (Czechoslovakia)	Jeannette Altwegg (Great Britain)	Yvonne Sherman (USA)
1951 Milan	Jeannette Altwegg (Great Britain)	Jacqueline du Bief (France)	Sonya Klopfer (USA)
1952 Paris	Jacqueline du Bief (France)	Sonya Klopfer (USA)	Virginia Baxter (USA)
1953 Davos	Tenley Albright (USA)	Gundi Busch (Germany)	Valda Osborn (Great Britain)
1954 Oslo	Gundi Busch (Germany)	Tenley Albright (USA)	Erica Batchelor (Great Britain)
1955 Vienna	Tenley Albright (USA)	Carol Heiss (USA)	Hanna Eigel (Austria)
1956 Garmisch	Carol Heiss (USA)	Tenley Albright (USA)	Ingrid Wendl (Austria)
1957 Colorado Springs	Carol Heiss (USA)	Hanna Eigel (Austria)	Ingrid Wendl (Austria)
1958 Paris	Carol Heiss (USA)	Ingrid Wendl (Austria)	Hanna Walter (Austria)
1959 Colorado Springs	Carol Heiss (USA)	Hanna Walter (Austria)	Sjoukje Dijkstra (Netherlands)
1960 Vancouver	Carol Heiss (USA)	Sjoukje Dijkstra (Netherlands)	Barbara Roles (USA)

1962 Prague	Sjoukje Dijkstra (Netherlands)	Wendy Griner (Canada)	Regine Heitzer (Austria)
1963 Cortina	Sjoukje Dijkstra (Netherlands)	Regine Heitzer (Austria)	Nicole Hassler (France)
1964 Dortmund	Sjoukje Dijkstra (Netherlands)	Regine Heitzer (Austria)	Petra Burka (Canada)
1965 Colorado Springs	Petra Burka (Canada)	Regine Heitzer (Austria)	Peggy Fleming (USA)
1966 Davos	Peggy Fleming (USA)	Gabriele Seyfert (East Germany)	Petra Burka (Canada)
1967 Vienna	Peggy Fleming (USA)	Gabriele Seyfert (East Germany)	Hana Maskova (Czechoslovakia)
1968 Geneva	Peggy Fleming (USA)	Gabriele Seyfert (East Germany)	Hana Maskova (Czechoslovakia)
1969 Colorado Springs	Gabriele Seyfert (East Germany)	Beatrix Schuba (Austria)	Zsuzsa Almassy (Hungary)
1970 Ljubljana	Gabriele Seyfert (East Germany)	Beatrix Schuba (Austria)	Julie Holmes (USA)
1971 Lyon	Beatrix Schuba (Austria)	Julie Holmes (USA)	Karen Magnussen (Canada)
1972 Calgary	Beatrix Schuba (Austria)	Karen Magnussen (Canada)	Janet Lynn (USA)
1973 Bratislava	Karen Magnussen (Canada)	Janet Lynn (USA)	Christine Errath (East Germany)
1974 Munich	Christine Errath (East Germany)	Dorothy Hamill (USA)	Dianne de Leeuw (Netherlands)
1975 Colorado Springs	Dianne de Leeuw (Netherlands)	Dorothy Hamill (USA)	Christine Errath (East Germany)
1976 Gothenburg	Dorothy Hamill (USA)	Christine Errath (East Germany)	Dianne de Leeuw (Netherlands)
1977 Tokyo	Linda Fratianne (USA)	Anett Pötzsch (East Germany)	Dagmar Lurz (West Germany)
1978 Ottawa	Anett Pötzsch (East Germany)	Linda Fratianne (USA)	Susanna Driano (Italy)
1979 Vienna	Linda Fratianne (USA)	Anett Pötzsch (East Germany)	Emi Watanabe (Japan)
1980 Dortmund	Anett Pötzsch (East Germany)	Dagmar Lurz (West Germany)	Linda Fratianne (USA)

Linda Fratianne, twice defeated Anett Pötzsch to win world crowns in 1977 and 1979. Anett turned the tables in the year between, their annual confrontations providing a succession of thrilling close-fought duels.

Emi Watanabe, renowned for her exotic style of presentation, made world championship history in Vienna in 1979 when she became the first Japanese girl to finish in the first three. Looking far from inscrutable, she cried with happiness when standing on the podium to receive her bronze medal.

Norris Bowden and Frances Dafoe, of Canada, won the world pair skating title twice, in 1954 and 1955, but were denied Olympic gold at Cortina d'Ampezzo, Italy, in 1956, when the Austrian winners, Kurt Oppelt and Sissy Schwarz, just managed to peg back the Canadians into close second place.

Pairs

	Gold	Silver	Bronze
1908 Leningrad	Heinrich Burger Anna Hübler (Germany)	James Johnson Phyllis Johnson (Great Britain)	L. Popowa A. Fischer (Russia)
1909 Stockholm	James Johnson Phyllis Johnson (Great Britain)	Nils Rosenius Valborg Lindahl (Sweden)	Richard Johanson Gertrud Ström (Sweden)
1910 Berlin	Heinrich Burger Anna Hübler (Germany)	Walter Jakobsson Ludowika Eilers (Finland)	James Johnson Phyllis Johnson (Great Britain)
1911 Vienna	Walter Jakobsson Ludowika Eilers (Finland)	— —	— —
1912 Manchester	James Johnson Phyllis Johnson (Great Britain)	Walter Jakobsson Ludowika Eilers (Finland)	Yngvar Bryn Alexia Schöyen (Norway)
1913 Stockholm	Karl Mejstrik Helene Engelmann (Austria)	Walter Jakobsson Ludowika Eilers (Finland)	Leo Horwitz Christa von Szabo (Austria)
1914 St Moritz	Walter Jakobsson Ludowika Eilers (Finland)	Karl Maejstrik Helene Engelmann (Austria)	Leo Horwitz Christa von Szabo (Austria)
1922 Davos	Alfred Berger Helene Engelmann (Austria)	Walter Jakobsson Ludowika Eilers (Finland)	Paul Metzner Margaret Metzner (Germany)
1923 Oslo	Walter Jakobsson Ludowika Eilers (Finland)	Yngvar Bryn Alexia Schöyen (Norway)	Kaj af Ekström Elna Henrikson (Sweden)
1924 Manchester	Alfred Berger Helene Engelmann (Austria)	John Page Ethel Muckelt (Great Britain)	Kaj af Ekström Elna Henrikson (Sweden)
1925 Vienna	Ludwig Wrede Herma Jaross-Szabo (Austria)	Pierre Brunet Andrée Joly (France)	Otto Kaiser Lilly Scholz (Austria)
1926 Berlin	Pierre Brunet Andrée Joly (France)	Otto Kaiser Lilly Scholz (Austria)	Ludwig Wrede Herma Jaross-Szabo (Austria)
1927 Vienna	Ludwig Wrede Herma Jaross-Szabo (Austria)	Otto Kaiser Lilly Scholz (Austria)	Oscar Hoppe Else Hoppe (Czechoslovakia)
1928 London	Pierre Brunet Andrée Joly (France)	Otto Kaiser Lilly Scholz (Austria)	Ludwig Wrede Melitta Brunner (Austria)
1929 Budapest	Otto Kaiser Lilly Scholz (Austria)	Ludwig Wrede Melitta Brunner (Austria)	Sandor Szalay Olga Organista (Hungary)
1930 New York	Pietre Brunet Andrée Joly (France)	Ludwig Wrede Melitta Brunner (Austria)	Sherwin Badger Beatrix Loughran (USA)
1931 Berlin	Lázló Szollás Emilie Rotter (Hungary)	Sandor Szalay Olga Organista (Hungary)	Karl Zwack Idi Papez (Austria)
1932 Montreal	Pierre Brunet Andrée Joly (France)	László Szollás Emilie Rotter (Hungary)	Sherwin Badger Beatrix Loughran (USA)
1933 Stockholm	László Szollás Emilie Rotter (Hungary)	Karl Zwack Idi Papez (Austria)	Chris Christensen Randi Bakke (Norway)
1934 Helsinki	László Szollás Emilie Rotter (Hungary)	Karl Zwack Idi Papez (Austria)	Ernst Baier Maxi Herber (Germany)

1935 Budapest	László Szollás Emilie Rotter (Hungary)	Erich Pausin Ilse Pausin (Austria)	Rezsö Dillinger Lucy Gallo (Hungary)
1936 Paris	Ernst Baier Maxi Herber (Germany)	Erich Pausin Ilse Pausin (Austria)	Leslie Cliff Violet Cliff (Great Britain)
1937 London	Ernst Baier Maxi Herber (Germany)	Erich Pausin Ilse Pausin (Austria)	Leslie Cliff Violet Cliff (Great Britain)
1938 Berlin	Ernst Baier Maxi Herber (Germany)	Erich Pausin Ilse Pausin (Austria)	Gunther Noack Inge Koch (Germany)
1939 Budapest	Ernst Baier Maxi Herber (Germany)	Erich Pausin Ilse Pausin (Austria)	Gunther Noack Inge Koch (Germany)
1947 Stockholm	Pierre Baugniet Micheline Lannoy (Belgium)	Peter Kennedy Karol Kennedy (USA)	Edmond Verbustel Suzanne Diskeuve (Belgium)
1948 Davos	Pierre Baugniet Micheline Lannoy (Belgium)	Ede Király Andrea Kékesy (Hungary)	Wallace Diestelmeyer Suzanne Morrow (Canada)
1949 Paris	Ede Király Andrea Kékesy (Hungary)	Peter Kennedy Karol Kennedy (USA)	Carleton Hoffner Ann Davies (USA)
1950 London	Peter Kennedy Karol Kennedy (USA)	John Nicks Jennifer Nicks (Great Britain)	Laszlo Nagy Marianne Nagy (Hungary)
1951 Milan	Paul Falk Ria Baran (Germany)	Peter Kennedy Karol Kennedy (USA)	John Nicks Jennifer Nicks (Great Britain)
1952 Paris	Paul Falk Ria Baran (Germany)	Peter Kennedy Karol Kennedy (USA)	John Nicks Jennifer Nicks (Great Britain)

Bob Paul and Barbara Wagner continued the Canadian pair skating glory initiated by Norris Bowden and Frances Dafoe. Bob and Barbara enjoyed four straight world wins, beginning in 1957, and topped them with an impressive Olympic victory at Squaw Valley, California, in 1960.

1953 Davos	John Nicks Jennifer Nicks (Great Britain)	Norris Bowden Frances Dafoe (Canada)	Laszlo Nagy Marianne Nagy (Hungary)
1954 Oslo	Norris Bowden Frances Dafoe (Canada)	Michel Grandjean Silvia Grandjean (Switzerland)	Kurt Oppelt Sissy Schwarz (Austria)
1955 Vienna	Norris Bowden Frances Dafoe (Canada)	Kurt Oppelt Sissy Schwarz (Austria)	Laszlo Nagy Marianne Nagy (Hungary)
1956 Garmisch	Kurt Oppelt Sissy Schwarz (Austria)	Norris Bowden Frances Dafoe (Canada)	Franz Ningel Marika Kilius (West Germany)
1957 Colorado Springs	Robert Paul Barbara Wagner (Canada)	Franz Ningel Marika Kilius (West Germany)	Otto Jelinek Maria Jelinek (Canada)
1958 Paris	Robert Paul Barbara Wagner (Canada)	Zdenek Dolezai Vera Suchankova (Czechoslovakia)	Otto Jelinek Maria Jelinek (Canada)
1959 Colorado Springs	Robert Paul Barbara Wagner (Canada)	Hans-Jürgen Bäumler Marika Kilius (West Germany)	Ronald Ludington Nancy Ludington (USA)
1960 Vancouver	Robert Paul Barbara Wagner (Canada)	Otto Jelinek Maria Jelinek (Canada)	Hans-Jürgen Bäumler Marika Kilius (West Germany)
1962 Prague	Otto Jelinek Maria Jelinek (Canada)	Oleg Protopopov Ludmila Belousova (USSR)	Franz Ningel Margret Göbl (West Germany)
1963 Cortina	Hans-Jürgen Bäumler Marika Kilius (West Germany)	Oleg Protopopov Ludmila Belousova (USSR)	Aleksandr Gavrilov Tatjana Zhuk (USSR)
1964 Dortmund	Hans-Jürgen Bäumler Marika Kilius (West Germany)	Oleg Protopopov Ludmila Belousova (USSR)	Guy Revell Debbi Wilkes (Canada)
1965 Colorado Springs	Oleg Protopopov Ludmila Belousova (USSR)	Ronald Joseph Vivian Joseph (USA)	Aleksandr Gorelik Tatjana Zhuk (USSR)
1966 Davos	Oleg Protopopov Ludmila Belousova (USSR)	Aleksandr Gorelik Tatjana Zhuk (USSR)	Ronald Kauffman Cynthia Kauffman (USA)
1967 Vienna	Oleg Protopopov Ludmila Belousova (USSR)	Wolfgang Danne Margot Glockshuber (West Germany)	Ronald Kauffman Cynthia Kauffman (USA)
1968 Geneva	Oleg Protopopov Ludmila Belousova (USSR)	Aleksandr Gorelik Tatjana Zhuk (USSR)	Ronald Kauffman Cynthia Kauffman (USA)

Otto and Maria Jelinek, the self-exiled Czechoslovak pair who represented Canada, ironically gaining a world victory in Prague in 1962. Canada and the United States insisted that they be readmitted to their old country 'without let or hindrance'. Otto subsequently became a Canadian member of parliament and is skating commentator on Canadian television.

1969 Colorado Springs	Alexsei Ulanov Irina Rodnina (USSR)	Alexsei Mishin Tamara Moskvina (USSR)	Oleg Protopopov Ludmila Belousova (USSR)
1970 Ljubljana	Alexsei Ulanov Irina Rodnina (USSR)	Andrei Suraikin Ludmila Smirnova (USSR)	Heinz Walther Heidemarie Steiner (East Germany)
1971 Lyon	Alexsei Ulanov Irina Rodnina (USSR)	Andrei Suraikin Ludmila Smirnova (USSR)	Kenneth Shelley Jo Jo Starbuck (USA)
1972 Calgary	Alexsei Ulanov Irina Rodnina (USSR)	Andrei Suraikin Ludmila Smirnova (USSR)	Kenneth Shelley Jo Jo Starbuck (USA)
1973 Bratislava	Aleksandr Zaitsev Irina Rodnina (USSR)	Alexsei Ulanov Ludmila Smirnova (USSR)	Uwe Kagelmann Manuela Gross (East Germany)
1974 Munich	Aleksandr Zaitsev Irina Rodnina (USSR)	Alexsei Ulanov Ludmila Smirnova (USSR)	Rolf Oesterreich Romy Kermer (East Germany)
1975 Colorado Springs	Aleksandr Zaitsev Irina Rodnina (USSR)	Rolf Oesterreich Romy Kermer (East Germany)	Uwe Kagelmann Manuela Gross (East Germany)
1976 Gothenburg	Aleksandr Zaitsev Irina Rodnina (USSR)	Rolf Oesterreich Romy Kermer (East Germany)	Aleksandr Vlasov Irina Vorobjeva (USSR)
1977 Tokyo	Aleksandr Zaitsev Irina Rodnina (USSR)	Aleksandr Vlasov Irina Vorobjeva (USSR)	Randy Gardner Tai Babilonia (USA)
1978 Ottawa	Aleksandr Zaitsev Irina Rodnina (USSR)	Uwe Bewersdorff Manuela Mager (East Germany)	Randy Gardner Tai Babilonia (USA)
1979 Vienna	Randy Gardner Tai Babilonia (USA)	Sergei Shakrai Marina Cherkasova (USSR)	Tassilo Thierbach Sabine Baesz (East Germany)
1980 Dortmund	Sergei Shakrai Marina Cherkasova (USSR)	Uwe Bewersdorff Manuela Mager (East Germany)	Stanislav Leonovich Malina Pestova (USSR)

Ice Dance

	Gold	Silver	Bronze
1952 Paris	Lawrence Demmy Jean Westwood (Great Britain)	John Slater Joan Dewhirst (Great Britain)	Daniel Ryan Carol Peters (USA)
1953 Davos	Lawrence Demmy Jean Westwood (Great Britain)	John Slater Joan Dewhirst (Great Britain)	Daniel Ryan Carol Peters (USA)
1954 Oslo	Lawrence Demmy Jean Westwood (Great Britain)	Paul Thomas Nesta Davies (Great Britain)	Edward Bodel Carmel Bodel (USA)
1955 Vienna	Lawrence Demmy Jean Westwood (Great Britain)	Paul Thomas Pamela Weight (Great Britain)	Raymond Lockwood Barbara Radford (Great Britain)
1956 Garmisch	Paul Thomas Pamela Weight (Great Britain)	Courtney Jones June Markham (Great Britain)	Gerard Rigby Barbara Thompson (Great Britain)
1957 Colorado Springs	Courtney Jones June Markham (Great Britain)	William McLachlan Géraldine Fenton (Canada)	Bert Wright Sharon McKenzie (USA)
1958 Paris	Courtney Jones June Markham (Great Britain)	William McLachlan Géraldine Fenton (Canada)	Donald Jacoby Andrée Anderson (USA)

Britain's Bernard Ford and Diane Towler, four times world title holders, were perhaps the most versatile ice dancers. They will be long remembered for their skillful interpretation of the film theme, 'Zorba the Greek,' for which they were constantly in demand during exhibitions. Both are now coaches, Bernard in Canada and Diane in England.

Year / Location			
1959 Colorado Springs	Courtney Jones Doreen Denny (Great Britain)	Donald Jacoby Andrée Anderson (USA)	William McLachlan Géraldine Fenton (Canada)
1960 Vancouver	Courtney Jones Doreen Denny (Great Britain)	William McLachlan Virginia Thompson (Canada)	Jean-Paul Guhel Christine Guhel (France)
1962 Prague	Pavel Roman Eva Romanova (Czechoslovakia)	Jean-Paul Guhel Christine Guhel (France)	William McLachlan Virginia Thompson (Canada)
1963 Cortina	Pavel Roman Eva Romanova (Czechoslovakia)	Michael Phillips Linda Shearman (Great Britain)	Kenneth Ormsby Paulette Doan (Canada)
1964 Dortmund	Pavel Roman Eva Romanova (Czechoslovakia)	Kenneth Ormsby Paulette Doan (Canada)	David Hickinbottom Janet Sawbridge (Great Britain)
1965 Colorado Springs	Pavel Roman Eva Romanova (Czechoslovakia)	David Hickinbottom Janet Sawbridge (Great Britain)	John Carrell Lorna Dyer (USA)
1966 Davos	Bernard Ford Diane Towler (Great Britain)	Dennis Sveum Kristin Fortune (USA)	John Carrell Lorna Dyer (USA)
1967 Vienna	Bernard Ford Diane Towler (Great Britain)	John Carrell Lorna Dyer (USA)	Malcolm Cannon Yvonne Suddick (Great Britain)
1968 Geneva	Bernard Ford Diane Towler (Great Britain)	Malcolm Cannon Yvonne Suddick (Great Britain)	Jon Lane Janet Sawbridge (Great Britain)
1969 Colorado Springs	Bernard Ford Diane Towler (Great Britain)	Aleksandr Gorshkov Ludmila Pakhomova (USSR)	James Sladky Judy Schwomeyer (USA)
1970 Ljubljana	Aleksandr Gorshkov Ludmila Pakhomova (USSR)	James Sladky Judy Schwomeyer (USA)	Erich Buck Angelika Buck (West Germany)
1971 Lyon	Aleksandr Gorshkov Ludmila Pakhomova (USSR)	Erich Buck Angelika Buck (West Germany)	James Sladky Judy Schwomeyer (USA)
1972 Calgary	Aleksandr Gorshkov Ludmila Pakhomova (USSR)	Erich Buck Angelika Buck (West Germany)	James Sladky Judy Schwomeyer (USA)
1973 Bratislava	Aleksandr Gorshkov Ludmila Pakhomova (USSR)	Erich Buck Angelika Buck (West Germany)	Glyn Watts Hilary Green (Great Britain)
1974 Munich	Aleksandr Gorshkov Ludmila Pakhomova (USSR)	Glyn Watts Hilary Green (Great Britain)	Gennadi Karponosov Natalia Linichuk (USSR)
1975 Colorado Springs	Andrei Minenkov Irina Moiseeva (USSR)	Jim Millns Colleen O'Connor (USA)	Glyn Watts Hilary Green (Great Britain)
1976 Gothenburg	Aleksandr Gorshkov Ludmila Pakhomova (USSR)	Andrei Minenkov Irina Moiseeva (USSR)	Jim Millns Colleen O'Connor (USA)
1977 Tokyo	Andrei Minenkov Irina Moiseeva (USSR)	Warren Maxwell Janet Thompson (Great Britain)	Gennadi Karponosov Natalia Linichuk (USSR)
1978 Ottawa	Gennadi Karponosov Natalia Linichuk (USSR)	Andrei Minenkov Irina Moiseeva (USSR)	Andras Sallay Krisztina Regöczy (Hungary)
1979 Vienna	Gennadi Karponosov Natalia Linichuk (USSR)	Andras Sallay Krisztina Regöczy (Hungary)	Andrei Minenkov Irina Moiseeva (USSR)
1980 Dortmund	Andras Sallay Krisztina Regöczy (Hungary)	Gennadi Karponosov Natalia Linichuk (USSR)	Andrei Minenkov Irina Moiseeva (USSR)

Index

Numbers in italics refer to captions and illustrations.

Aladdin 78
Albright, Tenley 68, *68*, 69
Allen, Scotty 71
Altwegg, Jeannette 31, 32, *33*, 68
Arabian Nights 75
Arnold, Tom 77, 78
Asche, Oscar 79

Babes in the Wood 79
Babilonia, Tai 50, 53, *53*, 55
Baier, Ernst 53, 68
Baird, John Logie 15
Ballets on Ice 75
Bartuschek, Leo 74
Baümler, Hans-Jürgen 52, *52*, 53, 71
Baxter, Virginia 68
Bearing, Frank 74
Beauchamp, Bobby 21, *21*
Belousova, Ludmila 19, *51*, 52-3, *70*, 71
Belita 76, *76*, 79
Berezowski, Barbara 46, *59*
Bief, Jacqueline du 20-21, *20*, 28, 68
Böckl, Willy 66
Boswell, Henry 9
Botticelli, Michael 46
Bowden, Norris 90
British Ice Dance Championships 26, 58
Brunet, Pierre 19, 66, 67
Buck, Angelika and Erich 60
Burger, Heinrich 64
Bushnell, E.W. 10
Button, Dick 28, 33, 39, *39*, 40, 68

Canadian Figure Skating Association 12, 19;
  Championships 39, 58
Chalfen, Morris 76
Chetverukhin, Sergei 72
Chu Chin Chow 79
Cinderella 78
Colledge, Cecilia 31-2, 45, 65, 77-8, *78*
Cosgrove, Mike 40
Coubertin, Pierre de 67, 68
Cousins, Robin 18, 35, 41, 45, 47, 49, 55
Cranston, Toller 47, *48*, 49, 72, 81
Curry, John 31-2, *42*, 47, 48-9, 72-3, 81, *85*

Dafoe, Frances 90
Dancing Years, The 81
Danzer, Emmerich 37, 71
death spiral 51-2, 71, 75
Deering, Margaret 22
Demmy, Lawrence *57*, 60
Dench, Robert 60
Denny, Doreen 60, *62*
Dick Whittington 79
Dietl, Fritz 33
Dijkstra, Sjoukje 71, *72*
Dillingham, Charles 74
Disney, Walt 70, 81
Divin, Carol 40, 71
Dodd, Patricia 31, 32
double racking 23

Elvin, Sir Arthur 79
Empress Hall 76, 78, 79, 81
Errath, Christine 46, *46*
European Figure Skating Championships
  19, 39
  Cologne 1973 47
  Helsinki 1977 54
  Zagreb 1979 55

Fassi, Carlo and Christa 33
Figure and Fancy Skating 12
figure eights 28, 30, 31
figures 16, 19, 22-3, 27-33, *34*, 57, 64, 68,
  69, 71, 73
  blades for *22*
  bracket *31*
  compulsory 26, 27, 28-33, *34*, 46
  international schedule of 29
  judging and marking 26, *27*, 30, 33, 34,
  46, 47, 73
  counter *30*, 31
  double three *30*, 31
  loop *30*, 31
  rocker *30*, 31
  scribes 33
  three *30*, 31
Fleming, Peggy 28, 37, 47-8, 71, 81
Ford, Bernard *24*, 26, 46, 60-61, *94*
Franks, Sheryl 46
Fratianne, Linda 89
free skating 22, 27, 28, 31, 32, 33, 34,
  43-9 *passim*, 50, 59, 62, 64, 68, 69, 71, 72
  blades for *22*, 23
  music for 43-6 *passim*
  see also short free; long free
Fryett, Stanley 74

Galbraith, Sheldon 39, 40-41
Gamgee, John 11
Gardner, Randy 50, 53, *53*, 55
Gerschwiler, Arnold 31
Gerschwiler, Jacques ('Gersch') 31, 32
Gilbert, Emery 76
Glaciarium 11, *18*
Goodfellow, Arthur 11
Gorshkov, Aleksandr 46, 60-61, *60*, 73
Grafström, Gillis 64-6, *67*, 68

Haines, Jackson 11, 14
Hamill, Dorothy *65*, 73
handicapped, skating for the 20-22
Harris, John H. 76
Hearne, Richard 78
Heiss, Carol 29, 31, 32, 69, 70
Herber, Maxie 12
Hoffmann, Jan 38, 41, *55*, 73
Holiday on Ice 76, 77, *77*, 81, *81*
Horne, Peri 60
Hot Ice 77
Hübler, Anna 64
Humpty Dumpty 80

Ice Capades 76, 77, 81
Ice Caprice 77
ice dancing 15, 23, 46, 50, 57-63

blades *22*, 23
chassé 59
choctaw 59
compulsory dances 58-9, 62
free dancing 58-9, 61-3
granted Olympic status 58, 73
kilian hold 60, *61*
set pattern dances 57-60
waltz hold 60, *61*
Ice Follies 75, 77, 81
Ice Parade 77
ice theatre 15, 43, 74-81
  arabesque 62
  ballet 74, 76, 77
  comedy acts 78, 80
  films 74-5
  musicals 75, 78, 81
  pantomime 78-9, 80-81
  revues 74, 75, 76, 78, 81
  TV spectaculars 81
Ice Vogues 78
Inge, Adele 78
International Olympic Committee 57, 70,
  71-2, 73
International Skating Union 12, 16, 19,
  28-9, 38, 40, 41, 43, 47, 56, 61, 63
  Congress (1903) 12
  Ice Dance Committee 63

Jackson, Donald 36, 39-40, 45
Jelinek, Otto and Maria 92
Jenkins, David 69, 70
Jenkins, Hayes 69, *82*
Johnson, Oscar 75
Joly, Andrée 19, 66, 67
Jones, Courtney 60, 62
judges 26, 27, 37, 47, 56, 63
  marking 37, 38, 40, 47, 50, 55-6, 59
  ISU scale 38, 47
jumps 11, 22, 28, 31, 34, 37, 38, 44, 46, 47,
  49, 55, 61, 63, 69, 71, 72
  axel 38-40, 44, 54, 75
  cherry, cherry flip *see* loop (toe)
  flip *see* salchow (toe)
  loops 37-8, 39, 49, 53, 68
  lutz 37-8, 39-40, 53
  salchow 37-8, 49, 54
  split 26, 37, 44
  three 37, 38
  triple 26, 40, 70
  walley 37-8

Karponosov, Gennadi *58*
Kauffman, Cynthia 55
Kauffman, Ronald 55
Keats, Eva 59, 60
Kelley, Susan 46
Kilius, Marika 52, *52*, 53, 71
Kirby, Michael 78
Kubicka, Terry 46

Langdon, Claude 75, 76, 78, 79
Leeuw, Diane de 73
Leskinen, Pekka 46

lifts 51, 54, 61, 62
  loop 53
  overhead axel 53
  quadruple 54
  split lutz 53, 71
  twists 53, 54
Linichuk, Natalia 58
linking steps 34, 46-7, 49, 50
London Coliseum 75, 76, 80
'long free' programme 46, 47, 50
Ludington, Ron 59
Lussi, Gustave 33, 39
Lynn, Janet 47, *72*, 73

Magnussen, Karen 72, 81, 88
Marina 75, 76
Markham, June 60
Maskova, Hana 45
McPherson, Donald 86
Midsummer Night's Dream (ballet) 77-8
Minenkov, Andrei 46
Moiseeva, Irina 46
Muckelt, Ethel 66

National Skating Association of Great
  Britain 11, 12
Nepela, Ondrej 71, *71*, 72
Nicks, Jennifer and John 55
Nord, Gloria 23-4, 79, 80
North American Championships 39
Novello, Ivor 81

Oelschlagel, Charlotte 74-5
Olympics 5, 15, 64-73
  1908 London *14*, 64
  1920 Antwerp 64
  1924 Chamonix 14, 19, 64, 66, 73
  1928 St Moritz 67
  1932 Lake Placid 67, *67*, 68
  1936 Garmisch-Partenkirchen 67-8
  1940 Sapporo (cancelled) 68
  1948 St Moritz 68
  1952 Oslo 32, 68
  1956 Cortina d'Ampezzo 68-9
  1960 Squaw Valley 15-16, 32, 69-71
  1964 Innsbruck 71, 72
  1968 Grenoble 52-3, 71-2
  1972 Sapporo 47, 72, 73
  1976 Innsbruck 49, 72
  1980 Lake Placid 73
  1984 Sarajevo 73
  ice dancing accepted 58
  recognition of figure skating 12, 64
  Summer Games (London 1908) 12, 64
  table of entries 73
One in a Million 15, 76
Owen, Laurence 15
Owen, Maribel Vinson 15
Owen, Maribel Jr. 15

pair skating 5, 12, 50-56, 61, 62, 63, 64,
  67, 75
Pakhomova, Ludmila 46, 60, *60*, 61, 73
Page, John 66
Palmer, Gerald 77, 79
Paul, Robert 70, *91*
Paulsen, Axel 11, 38
Pausin, Erich and Ilse 68
Pepys, Samuel 8, 57
Perren, Armand 77

Porter, David 46, *59*
Pötzsch, Anett *35*
Prince's Skating Club 12, 64
Protopopov, Oleg 19, *51*, 52-3, *70*. 71

Richardson, Capt. T.D. 14
rinks 18, 26
  artificial 11, 12, 14, 19, 26, 74
  indoor 10-11, 14, 16, 19, 64
  modern outdoor *17*
  old style *14*
  permanent 19
  portable 74, 77, 81
Robertson, Ronnie 69
Rodnina, Irina 47, *50*, 53-4, 55, *56*, 72, 73
Roman, Pavel 60, 63
Romanova, Eva 60, 63
Rose Marie 78-9, *79*

Salchow, Ulrich 11, 12, 38, 64, 66
Schäfer, Karl 57, 68
Schnelldorfer, Manfred 71
Schöller, Franz 57
Schreiter, Karl 58, 60
Schuba, Trixi 31, *32*, 32-3, 72
Schwarz, Wolfgang 71
Schwomeyer, Judy 59
Scott, Barbara Ann *34*, 68, 78, *79*
Seyfert, Gabriele 69, 71
shadow (mirror) skating 50, 63
Shakrai, Sergei 54, *54*
Sharp, Graham 67, *82*
Shipstad, Eddie and Roy 75
'short free' programme 5, 28, 46-7, 50
Skaters Text Book 12
skates, skating
  as recreation 7
  as transport 7, 8
  boots and 11, 22-3, 24-5
  development of 7-9, 10
  figure 22, *22*
  blades 22-4, *22*, *24*, *29*
  care of 23, 24-5
  toe pick (rake) 22, *23*, 62
  guards 22, *24*
Skating 11, 56
Sladky, James 59
Smirnova, Ludmila 72
Snow White and the Seven Dwarfs 81
spins 22, 26, 28, 31, 34, 37, 40, 44, 46,
  47, 49, 61
  arabesque *see* camel
  camel 35, 62, 75
  catch-waist 53
  cross-foot 35-6, 44
  death *51*, 51-2, 71, 75
  flying 66
  in pairs 51
  Kauffman 55
  music for 46
  positions 34
  sit 11, *35*, 44, 53
  spirals 28, 34, 44, 47, 49
  spread eagle 34, 44
Stars on Ice 78
St Moritz 76
Stoll Theatre 75, 77, 78
Stroukoff, Andrew 46
Suraikin, Andrei 72
Syers, Edgar 64

Syers, Madge 12, 64
Szabó, Herma Plank- 66

tank *see* rink, portable
Taylor, Megan 87
Taylor, Vern 40
Cherkasova, Marina 54, *54*, 55
television 5, 15, 16, 28, 47, 64, 69
  spectaculars 81
Thompson, Leonard 77
Three Rookies, the 78
throws (pairs) 51
  axel 54, 55
  salchow 54, 55
Tickner, Charles 45, *45*
Tomlins, Freddie 67
Towler, Diane *24*, 26, 46, 60-61, 94
Treatise on Skating, A 8
Tschaikowskaja, Elena 60
Turner, Lesley 60
Tyson, George 76

Ulanov, Alexsei 72, 73
United States 10, 15, 19, 21, 28, 32, 58,
  74, 75, 76, 81
  ice dancing championships 58
United States Figure Skating Association
  12, 15, 39

Vrzanova, Aja *32*
Vandervell, Henry F. 11
Vienna Ice Skating Club 11, 58
Vienna Skating School 68
Vinson, Maribel 75
Volkov, Sergei 73

Watanabe, Emi 89
Wagner, Barbara 70, *91*
Walker, Daphne 45, 78
Walley, Nat 38
Wallis, Daphne 60
Weld, Theresa 66
Wembley 78, *79*, 81
Westover Ice Rink (Bournemouth) 75
Westwood, Jean *57*, 60
Weyden, Eric Van der 59, 60
Whitton, Harry 21-2
Wilkie, Reginald 60
Witté, Hans 74
World Figure Skating Championships 12, 15
  19, 27, 50, 55, 64, *71*, 73
  1896 Leningrad 12
  1937 Vienna 31
  1952 Paris 21
  1960 Vancouver 16, 31
  1962 Prague 15, 39
  1964 Dortmund 53
  1965, 52
  1972 Calgary 32
  1973 Bratislava 54
  1975, 73
  1978 Ottawa 40
  1979 Vienna 5, 40
World Ice Dance Championships 26, 46
  1952 Paris 58, 60
World Junior Championships 21, 41
  1979 Augsburg 21, 41

Zayak, Elaine 21
Zaitsev, Aleksandr 47, *50*, 53-4, 55, *56*, 73